Praying Through Your Midnight

by
DR. ROSIE MESSENGER

I0151202

Published by:
LIVING IMAGE PUBLISHING LLC

Chicago, IL

Copyright @ 2015.   All rights reserved.
ISBN 978-0-9818732-3-7
Cover design: Living Image Publishing LLC

Proofreader: Romie M. Jackson

All rights reserved International Copyright Law. Content and or cover cannot be reproduced in any means, electronically or mechanical, including photocopying, recording or by any information storage and retrieval system, without written consent of Living Image Publishing LLC, Chicago, IL.

To book for events contact Dr. Rosie Messenger at Da' Bre Na Ministries; www.rosiemessenger.com.

Table of Contents

Preface

The Purpose

This writing is to show that prayer changes people, locations and situations.

The Scope

The project is written to return prayer to the forefront of ministry by presenting tools and strategies that will function in midnight situations so that one will not throw in the towel. The project covers all aspects of ministry, ministry workers, laity and the general churched and un-churched population. Although the level of truthful dialogue or sincere responses are out of my control, it is the concern of this author that males, females, especially teens and younger children, professionals and all humanity will include prayer in their daily activities, play habits, relationships, interactions and community involvement. Various churched and un-churched participants were interviewed using an assessment survey form related to seemingly hopeless situations to discover that praying through their midnight will produce joy in daylight.

It is written to help others understand and articulate the importance of praying during times of trouble and other adverse situations. Thus, the information contained in this writing will minister to specific needs during turbulent and dark times in an individual's life. It is a personal challenge to attempt to discover how lives are awakened and changed resulting from a clear understanding of a prayerful relationship with the Lord Jesus.

What if I do pray? Then you, the reader, can understand the spiritual dynamics of a solid prayer life. I want to show that when praying for release, relief and refocusing, something will happen. It is praying while using weapons of warfare that total deliverance will occur. It is time to press through your midnight in prayer. Know that midnight is a time of turmoil. It is between night and day. It may be lonely, but you are not alone at midnight. JESUS IS AWAKE!

What if you pray? Prayer causes the looming darkness to become transparent. Midnight experiences will serve to decrease stress and reshape every negative experience into positive experiences because your prayers before the Lord will never die. They are kept before God forever. The prayers prayed by your parents continue to live before God, today.

Evidence, challenges to hypothesis, historical background, contemporary text, definitions, principles and comparisons, analogies and direct support are addressed through testimonies, research, seminary teachings, personal Bible study, various classes and personal experiences have shaped each chapter and assignment of this writing. Prayers have reshaped history, changed the earth and set angels in motion on behalf of God's praying saints.

…the Bible teaches God answers prayer (Gen. 25:21; 2 Sam. 24:25; Ezra 8:23; Neh. 2:1; Acts 10:30-31). Here is an example of God answering prayer.

2 Kings 20:1-6 (NASB) In those days Hezekiah became mortally ill. And Isaiah the prophet the son of Amoz came to him and said to him, "Thus says the Lord, 'Set your house in order, for you shall die and not live.' " [2] Then he turned his face to the wall and prayed to the Lord, saying, [3] "Remember now, O Lord, I beseech You, how I have walked before You in truth and with a whole heart and have done what is good in Your sight." And Hezekiah wept bitterly. [4] Before Isaiah had gone out of the middle court, the word of the Lord came to him, saying, [5] "Return and say to Hezekiah the leader of My people, 'Thus says the Lord, the God of your father David, "I have heard your prayer, I have seen your tears; behold, I will heal you. On the third day you shall go up to the house of the Lord. [6] "I will add fifteen years to your life, and I will deliver you and this city from the hand of the king of Assyria; and I will defend this city for My own sake and for My servant David's sake." God tells Hezekiah, through the prophet Isaiah, that he is soon going to die from this illness. Hezekiah prays and the text says God heard his prayers and grants him an additional 15 years. What is interesting is Hezekiah didn't pray for a longer life but reminded God how he walked in truth and did what is good in God's sight. God saw Hezekiah's tears and heard his prayers and gave him the answer he truly desired but didn't directly ask for. Does prayer change things? God does the changing but He uses our prayers as part of the process. Through answered prayer God gave Hezekiah a longer life. The Bible has multiple examples of answered prayer, which should give us confidence to pray.[1]

Contextually, of the many sources referenced, one fact stands

Praying
through
Your Midnight

From dissapointments, adversities, relationships, health issues... to Life, Joy and Peace

Faith

Godly Counsel

Holy Spirit Worship

Continual Prayer

Dr. Rosie Messenger

out, "The Lord Restores Me." Consistently, restoration is summarized as follows: "You press me down, the Lord picks me up; you criticize my actions; He approves my ways; you plant snares, but He restores me; you don't understand the cause; you don't know why; you cry out in agony; you wonder where God is…But He restores you. Like David, He is our rod and staff. Like Paul, He is our conversion. Like Moses, He is our burning bush on the back side of the dessert. Like Elias, He is our mantle; Like Habakkuk, He is our faithful vision because the "Lord is our Shepherd and He Restores Us".

My claim is that "Prayer changes people, locations and situations" and Midnight is:

- A time of darkness and un-certainty

- A time of depression and feeling down

- A time of questioning: God are you listening?

- A time of pain and suffering that may be filled with unhealthy thoughts

- A time when one is drowning at the peak of dawn

- A time to disarm the enemy through prayer

- A time of overwhelming grief and sorrow

- A time to say, "hello dawn, my midnight is over"

My reason for writing this work is to show that prayer works and to show how it has worked to improve relationships, shape character, restore trust, change mental perspectives and enable one to go places one has never been.

My evidence is based on personal results and other witnessed results, other's testimonies, observed changes and deliverance during altar call prayer, survey forms results, the resolution of adverse medical conditions, changed lives, lives spared, community changes, acquisition of properties for ministry use (with no money) and many other changes in all areas of life. Hebrews 13:8 teaches that we serve an unchangeable God during changing times. If God was a changeable God, our standards would become compromised, creating an unstable environment that results in disobedient living. People change, time changes. We change mentally, physically, spiritually and culturally. Trouble changes people. God moves people to change trouble into testimonies. But, God is changeless---the same "yesterday and today."

How are my reasons relevant to my claim? Christianity's focus is to inspire belief through careful textual exegeses. The great prayer warrior, E. M. Bounds declares that "the most important lesson we can learn is how to pray."[2] (E. M. Bounds on Prayer, p.11). According to PEW Research Center's Forum, 2008, religion is very important in people's lives. On a national average, 56% of individuals based on a 46 state (smaller states combined) survey, believes in prayer and attends church. For example, in Illinois 56%, Alaska 37% and Mississippi 82% are in regular church attendance. In addition, a new analysis by the *Pew Research Center's Forum* on Religion & Public Life finds that African-Americans are markedly more religious on a variety of measures in the U.S. population as a whole as follows: Examples cited: 90% of African Americans have an absolute certain belief in God with a total U.S. population belief of 70%; a total of about 78% of African Americans admits that they pray at least daily with about 58% of the population.[3] (Pew, 2008)

Dedication

This book is dedicated to the memory of my mother, Ella Mae Perry, my brothers and sisters, and my church family (Holy Rock Church & Outreach Ministries). Most importantly, this book is dedicated to you, the reader, who may be struggling with one or multiple difficulties in your life. It is my prayer that you will discover the love of Jesus during your "Midnight Experience" and discover a renewed hope through Jesus based on the information contained in this writing.

This is a book that was initiated in 2012 as a personal journal in preparation for integration into book form. Read it prayerfully, do the exercises at the conclusion of each chapter and pass it on.

Acknowledgments

I am grateful to Jesus Christ, Our Savior for His provisions. He has provided me with a gentle giant of a husband (Apostle H. L. Messenger) who has been instrumental and supportive toward the completion of my terminal degree in ministry. Because of him, my strenuous educational plight has been a source of ministry learning joy.

In addition, I am grateful to the Royal Family of Holy Rock Church & Outreach Ministries for their endless prayers and support.

Also, I would be remiss if I failed to acknowledge the encouragement and the "go ahead" lectures from our friends, Pastor Herbert Lee, Jr. and wife Naomi Lee. Thank you for your prayers!

Dr. Rosie Messenger

Abbreviations

KJV	King James Version of the Bible
ESV	English Standard Version of the Bible
RSV	Revised Standard Version of the Bible
Gk	Greek
V/V.V	Verse
P.	Page

THE OLD TESTAMENT

Genesis	Gen.
Exodus	Exod.
Deuteronomy	Deut.
Judges	Judg.
1 & 11 Samuel	Sam.
Psalms	Ps./Psa.
Proverbs	Prov.
Ezekiel	Ezek.

THE NEW TESTAMENT

Matthew	Matt./Mt.
Mark	Mark
Romans	Rom.
1&2 Corinthians	Cor./Corin.
Galatians	Gal.
Ephesians	Eph.
Philippians	Phip.
1 & 2 Timothy	Tim.
Hebrews	Heb.
1 & 2 Peter	Pet.
Revelation	Rev.

1

Praying While Others Are Asleep? Who Needs Prayer?

Handle the Word:

Handle God's Word, pick it up and read;

Open His God-inspired book, check it out, and take a good look.

Handle His teachings "what does it say?"

It says, "Read, learn, walk and obey."

Embrace Him, feel the scar in His side;

Touch Him and as His love abide

Handle God's Word, pick it up and read;

Follow His ways, then you will in life succeed.

Handle the Word once in a while;

Use it to solve problems, it's sure to bring to your heart a smile

Handle the Word, it delivers, breaks yokes and brings forth new life;

Digest the Word of God, it rapidly dissipates hurt, suffering and strife

(By R. Messenger-1997)

Praying While Others are Asleep? Who Needs Prayer?

This book, on *praying through your midnight,* is written to help others understand and articulate the importance of praying during times of trouble, instances of struggle and other adverse situations. The hope is that the information shared in this writing will minister to needs during life's turbulent and dark times. The intention is to discover and share how lives are awakened and changed due to a clear understanding of a prevailing and prayerful relationship with the Lord so that you, the reader may understand the spiritual dynamics of a solid prayer life.

Thus, the approaching darkness that results from midnight experiences serves to reshape our negative experiences through prayer. To this end, prayer will challenge people, locations and situations based on historical background, contemporary text, definitions and principles of prayer as evidenced through direct and truthful testimonies. The context documents the reason for agreement based on sources. The sources are selected based on credible experiences and willingness and agreement to share written information related to a consistent prayer life.

The reason the subject of prayer was selected to present personal experiences and observed improvement in relationships that shaped character, restored trust, changed mental perspectives that enables one to go to places they have never dreamed they could go. Again, the evidence is also based on written surveys, personal observations, testimonies of deliverance and changed lives for the better. Only prayer could have ushered the changes to the forefront as demonstrated through active ministries in motion.

My reason is relevant to this writer's claim that one can pray through their midnight based on a Christianity that is God-focused with an inspired belief through exegetical teaching from the Biblical Text that prayer works. The Biblical Text supports prayer and faith as a way of dealing with times of darkness and despair. Because of this, one is able to pray through their midnights.

We doze off, but God never sleeps. It was said by the Psalmist in the days of old that "God never sleeps" because He is the watchman for our soul. He never slumbers during the night, therefore, there is no reason for us to worry through our midnight. To all who pray and become a willing seeker, he is a keeper. We are to try Him and stand firm on His Holy Word. To the midnight sufferer, He is always on His post. He fills us with the Holy Spirit, cures our doubts and calms our fears. Lean on Him and let Him work through ceaseless prayer.

Prayer Changes People

This writer stands on the premises that throughout Biblical

history, prayer has changed lives and set people on a steady course of correct thinking. The acceptance of ideas, theories, goals and purposes begins with a thought generated from a made-up mind to accept Jesus as the personal Savior. The psychiatrist specializes in reshaping the thought process, confronting past experiences, and changing how one views himself, their situations and exploring the reason for certain actions. When the pattern of erroneous thinking is changed, people will change. It is the same with Salvation. First, believe that the gospel message is true, then apply the message to your life, and finally, observe for change. Reflect back to your childhood. Can you recall that someone told you that they were praying for you or your family? Did it have an effect on your life? It's your turn; try prayer!

Prayer Changes Locations

Often times, prayer will change a person's location in order to change their direction. To remain in the same place, under the same conditions may be hazardous to one's health (spiritually and/or physically).   Lives have been spared because a person missed a flight. Thus, remained in a specific location. A missed train or bus has caused one to bypass serious injury from an accident, because that person remained in place. Relocation to another city, a job change, a route to work change, a school change, etc. has spared and shaped many lives. Prayerful change of location inspires and moves people toward their

God purposed destinations.

Prayer Changes Situations

It is common knowledge that prayer changes situations. According to recorded incidents, accidents and evil intents, prayer has changed a multitude of situations. Prayer has changed the course of mighty rivers that were on a steady course of destruction. The rising and raging waters were headed toward homes and would have destroyed homes and lives. Prayer has changed the direction of deadly tornadoes. There are countless stories detailing how prayer changed financial situations, marital relationships, hearts of evil men and the mind of a serial killer who regained peace from a confused state of mind. During a violent tornado in 2012, one person relays a story of how she locked herself in a small closet and prayed. Consequently, her entire home was destroyed, but not the closet from which she was praying. It remained standing in the midst of a completely destroyed home.

Assignment

- Describe how you measure the effectiveness of your prayer.
- Explain what the voice of the Holy Spirit is like in relation to your prayer life.
- Give an example of how prayer impacts your family structure and make up.
- Describe how prayer has changed your location, situation or the people around you.

2

Prayer, What Is It?

The Secret is out

What can God do? The secret is out;

He is the Father of Jesus; is there any doubt?

God sent Jesus as a replacement for my sins;

Oh, He sent kings, but it took more than could be done by any men

Jesus went to a secret place to pray, "Lord let this cup pass me by";

But the Father knew that when it seemed that He was afar off

He heard our mother's intercessory prayer

Now, the secret is out. He is alive and well.

He has freed us from the jaws of hell.

Of course, there is no secret what God can do, but once and for all, the secret is out.

Now, hear and witnesses what He is doing for you

(By R. Messenger, 1995)

Prayer; What is it?

Prayer is the process of developing an understanding of who God is, His plans for your life, His Holiness and your destiny, His plans and your salvation, and His plans to commune with Him as the Triune God. Prayer speaks to how God is spoken too about your service in His Kingdom. The way to become relational with Him is to develop communication with Him to the point that you trust, listen and obey what He is saying to you through prayer.

For Christians, prayer should be like taking a breath. Breathing is automatic. It is not pre-planned and does not require thought. The carbon dioxide builds up in the lungs via circulation and sets the brain into automatic motion that causes internal pressure to build up in the respiratory cavity and the requirement for oxygen causes breathing to simply "happen". If you are not totally convinced, attempt to hold your breath for longer than a "normal" time length. That is a task that must be practiced repeatedly before it is mastered. Yet, born again family members enter the realm of God and enjoy His Presence. His Holiness causes a loving pressure to build and push forth Spiritual refreshment over your life through prayer, praise and worship. Prayer become spontaneous, like the breathing process. Like the buildup of carbon dioxide in the system, the pressures of life mount and we automatically begin a prayer dialogue with Jesus. As you pray, it is easier to detect other's prayers. The collective mounting of prayer saturates the atmosphere with prayers that sets Jesus in motion on our behalf. "As believers we have all entered the divine atmosphere to breathe the air of prayer. Only then can we survive in the darkness of the world".[1]

The Purpose of Prayer

The purpose of prayer is to promote Christ-Centered growth by loving God with all of your might, soul and strength. This love must be communicated from the inside to the outside via the Holy Spirit through prayer. Like a spouse or a best friend, the more we know about them, the better the relationship becomes. The more we understand, the better our understanding.

Prayer completes us in Christ (Colossians 2:10). We are incomplete because we are searching for something (or someone) to fill the emptiness in our lives. Instead of filling life's voids with women, affairs, fame, praise, power, success, secrets, and other ungodly people or things, we are to seek completeness through Jesus Christ. How does one become complete? Completeness comes from the following:

1. Belief and trust in God and His Son Jesus – Redemptive work
2. Acceptance of Jesus Christ as God's Son and your Savior
3. Reliance on the Lord for solutions to your situations
4. Seeking to become filled with the Holy Spirit
5. Reverentially fearing God and in all our ways honor Him

6. By walking in advance victory (call those things that are not as if they have happened)

7. By not chasing after things of this world; let God do it, He will bring it to you;

8. By asking God for favor with the right people

9. Learn and know who you are in Christ;

10. View yourself as complete in Christ;

11. Develop an understanding of righteousness, holiness, and immolate Christ's character. Duplicate his ways

12. Allow faith to take lead in your life, no matter what

13. Believe and know with assurance that God loves you, no matter what

14. Believe God's love through prayer and meditation

15. Do not worry about others who do not value you or the Jesus you serve

16. Know that a relationship with you is something to be greatly desired and appreciated by others (because of righteousness, holiness and Christ's character in you)

17. Identify with Jesus, not with the people who may reject, criticize or judge you **LIVE TO PLEASE GOD, NOT PEOPLE.** To accomplish completeness through Christ requires a constant and consistent prayer life. It requires prayer and practice.

The Effect of Prayer

Prayer is like salt. Salt is sometimes used as an antiseptic. Bacteria is unable to survive in a salt water solution. The Word of God is like salt. It acts as a powerful antiseptic against Satan's kingdom. Like Salt, prayers are seasoned. Prayers will preserve us for kingdom work. Constant prayer manifests itself in ministry. Through a study in the Word, we gain a deep understanding of how the enemy operates and responds to a prayer of Holy salt solution. There is no need to go to the Priest to confess your sins so that He can relay them to Mary so she can tell her Son Jesus and Jesus tells his heavenly Father. We have direct access to Jesus Christ. GLORY TO GOD! Prayer is freely made in the Name of Jesus. It changes the aim. The aim becomes set on purity with a vision that is plain. Life becomes destiny-focused. We walk toward Him that sent us.

Like the victories that were won between Jerusalem and Edom over the Edomites, we are fighting sin and Satan. Prayer and faith are a victorious combination and it is the voice of victory, the air of praise, the joy of thanksgiving and the anticipation of worship that presents our gift of worship before Him, in His presence.

Prayer effects every component of life. It requires prayer and commitment to receive Christ Jesus as our PERSONAL Savior so that we may walk in Him (that pleases God) and become rooted and built up in Him (always thank Him), to know that we are complete in Him (He is the head). So that we may put off the sinful flesh and be buried in baptism and raised with Him through faith. We are to pray without ceasing because prayer changes things, people, places and situations.

To Change

Prayer facilitates growth, if it is practiced. When there is no self-love, usually there is no God-love. You are accustomed to "you". You are visible to "yourself". You are with "yourself" twenty-four (24) hours, seven (7) days a week. You look at "yourself" in the mirror, hear "yourself" speak, know your own private thoughts and true feelings and you know the places you like to go. Therefore you know "yourself" better than anyone else, with the exception of God, the creator of "yourself". With that in mind, you are aware of areas that requires improvement. If you could improve on your own, you would, but you cannot do it without God's intervention. So, if you do not love "yourself", do you love a loving God? If you do not like how you were born, try the New Birth, because it takes the Holy Spirit or a Spirit filled person to assist us to see and deal with our "self-issues."

To Enlighten

Change is enlightening, especially if it is discovered and presented by a person who is prayerfully connected to Jesus and His righteousness. Regular prayer and Scripture study in combination with listening to God will engage and enlighten our lives so we can engage in praise, worship and a life-style designed to glorify God. Prayer leads to praise, praise leads to worship and worship into the realm of God. We serve a God who desires to have us pray because He answers our prayers, especially when we pray in faith, trusting in His Word and treating others right. During prayer, we make requests known without doubting that God is all wise, all knowing and all seeing. Also, the Word enlightens and illuminates understanding of what is contained in the Bible and to improve our lives.

To Build Up the Body of Christ

Prayer must not become routine. Just as a baby grows and his/her body changes, so does a person grow in Christ and change. The child requires a different type of food as he/she becomes older, because milk alone does not satisfy the appetite or the body's requirement for nourishments. It takes an upward transition from milk to baby food, to toddler baby food to table food. So the Body of Christ is growing and developing individually. We all begin as "babes in Christ." Yet, we have the propensity to grow. The only way to grow is to ingest a regular diet of age appropriate foods. Unfortunately, we are unable to survive on milk or bread alone. Thus, not only does it take prayer, we are to have faith, trust, praise, worship and the Word. The Word ministered will help us address the areas of strengths and weaknesses. The Body of Christ has a need to be nourished from the Word, to grow. Once we are built up, we can assist with the work on someone else's building because we have become experienced building engineers. The goal is discipleship replication

"Lord, teach us to pray!" This request from one of the disciples (Luke 11:1) gave evidence of real spiritual insight. We must learn

how to pray. While praying is as natural to the Christian as breathing is to a mammal, even breathing must be studied and practiced if it is to be correct. Singers and public speakers work on their breathing so that they get the most out of their voice and don't injure it. The fact that we have been praying since childhood is no guarantee that we really know how to pray effectively.[2]

Examples of Prayers From the Biblical Text

The Biblical Text is filled with prayer of inspiration, adoration, confession, thanksgiving, affirmation, repentance, intercession, and requests. For examples, Psalms 11:4 details a prayer of confession, Psalms 8:1 presents a compelling prayer of confession, and I Corinthians discloses a prayer of petition. God is ready to hear a sincere prayer from a repentant heart. God does not score you on the type of prayer, but on the sincerity of prayer from a righteous heart. He will continue to teach you how to pray as long as you are sincere. Midnight prayer is praying through your storm. Storms are debilitating, expected and unexpected. The onset may be sudden or subtle. It brings wind, hail, rain, flooding, thunder and lightning. Its results may be devastating, but the survivors are able to rebuild and move on. Prayer affords us the ability to "move on" in-spite of people, places, situations or locations.

David's storm: Psalm 51 presents David's prayer of repentance that asks God to create in him (David) a clean heart, O God. David experienced an expected storm because he had been warned in a parable after the incident of him sleeping with another man's wife (Bathsheba) by the Prophet Nathan. David immediately realized that a storm was

brewing and he was unable to stop it. When the Lord sends a storm

your way, and you know it, it is time to put on sackcloth and fall on the

ash heap and pray. This is David's prayer from Psalm 51:1-19:

> *Have mercy on me, O God, according to your steadfast love; according to your abundant mercy blot out my transgressions. Wash me thoroughly from my iniquity, and cleanse me from my sin!*

> *For I know my transgressions, and my sin is ever before me. Against you, you only, have I sinned and done what is evil in your sight, so that you may be justified in your words and blameless in your judgment. Behold, I was brought forth in iniquity, and in sin did my mother conceive me. Behold, you delight in truth in the inward being, and you teach me wisdom in the secret heart.*

> *Purge me with hyssop, and I shall be clean; wash me, and I shall be whiter than snow. Let me hear joy and gladness; let the bones that you have broken rejoice. Hide your face from my sins, and blot out all my iniquities.*

> *Create in me a clean heart, O God, and renew a right spirit within me. Cast me not away from your presence, and take not your Holy Spirit from me. Restore to me the joy of your salvation, and uphold me with a willing spirit.*

> *Then I will teach transgressors your ways, and sinners will ³ʳreturn to you. Deliver me from blood guiltiness, O God, God of my salvation, and my tongue will sing aloud of your righteousness. O Lord, open my lips, and my mouth will declare your praise. For you will not delight in sacrifice, or I would give it; you will not be pleased with a burnt offering. The sacrifices of God are a broken spirit; a broken and contrite heart, O God, you will not despise.*

> *Do good to Zion in your good pleasure; build up the walls of Jerusalem; then will you delight in right sacrifices, in burnt offerings and whole burnt offerings; then bulls will be offered on your altar. (ESV Bible)*

In this text, David knew that he had sinned. Also, he knew that sin would corrupt because of its ungodly nature. Sin plays tricks on the imagination and desires of man. David had acted foolishly. The text portrays the characteristics of fools as those with no regard for Christian living or the gospel. Fools do not trust God and show a lack of knowledge for His ways. Fools act in an ungodly manner (Jeremiah 4:22; Isaiah 32:6). Fools fall prey to their own anger as Proverbs 29:11 teaches. Of course, fools are disobedient (Proverbs 10:8) and despise instruction and discipline (Jeremiah 18:12).

David confessed, repented and returned to the Lord. He asked to be purged with bitter hyssop. Hyssop is a plant (I Kings 4:33) that was used for extensive rituals for purification. It was used at the crucifixion (John 19:28-33). In other words, it was used as a cleansing agent for purification when sprinkled. Otherwise, he wanted a bundle of hyssop to be used to cleanse him because the bundle works together as one to do the job. It takes a bundle of hyssop to cleanse, but it takes one TRIUNE God to save, purge and cleanse from the inside out. David desired to have his inner being, mind, and faults purged. He examined himself and convicted himself of sin and desired forgiveness.

The major emphasis of Psalms is to learn to commune, communicate and compel God to our case. David asked for mercy

because he had sinned before God and his brethren. He asked God
to blot out or white out his transgressions and wash him from his
sins. David sought forgiveness as he prostrated himself on his face
in prayer. He demonstrated his brokenness by not wearing his stately
attire, but wearing sackcloth and fasting. What did God do for David? He restored his joy and removed his guilt. What did David do?
He praised God in adoration through musical instruments, dancing,
thanksgiving and song. He had experienced a soul cleansing.

This is important, review the steps David performed.

1. In prayer David admitted how great his sins were and gave an offering for his sin: "I was born in sin and shaped in iniquity."

2. He acknowledges that he knows God and God's desire, but he still made a sinful mistake.

3. He admitted that he strayed from the truth.

4. He knew that God could re-create him, make him whole and make him to know wisdom.

5. He requested a renewed spirit so that he could hear joy, be glad and have it all to exit from a clean heart.

6. David worshiped and praised God for his deliverance

Jesus' Example of Prayer

The Lord's Prayer: Luke 11:1-4 "*Now Jesus was praying in a certain place, and when he finished, one of his disciples said to him, "Lord, teach us to pray, as John taught his disciples." And he said to them, "When you pray, say: "Father, hallowed be your name. Your kingdom come. Give us each day our daily bread, and forgive us our sins, for we ourselves forgive everyone who is indebted to us. And lead us not into temptation." He called his disciples and his disciples responded by later calling on Jesus to "teach them how to pray."*

The disciples followed Jesus and learned that His examples of servant-hood and self-denial were astonishing. Jesus endured suffering (Matthew 10:24-25), served others, was faithful, loved everyone, patient, forgiving of others, was gentle and humble, exemplified purity and always prayed. God desires that his people will follow Jesus' examples and become conformed to His image. Therefore, the components of the Lord's Prayer are as follows:

A. Recognize that God is the Father and Lord (Luke 10:21)

B. Ask for and seek for God's perfect will for your life

C. Request physical provisions and forgiveness

D. Ask for spiritual protection, and

E. Learn about the kingdom of God

Paul's Example of Prayer

Paul's Visions and His Thorn: 12:2:-10 I know a man in Christ who fourteen years ago was caught up to the third heaven—whether in the body or out of the body I do not know, God knows. And I know that this man was caught up into paradise—whether in the body or out of the body I do not know, God knows— and he heard things that cannot be told, which man may not utter. On behalf of this man I will boast, but on my own behalf I will not boast, except of my weaknesses. Though if I should wish to boast, I would not be a fool, for I would be speaking the truth. But I refrain from it, so that no one may think more of me than he sees in me or hears from me. So to keep me from becoming conceited because of the surpassing greatness of the revelations, a thorn was given me in the flesh, a messenger of Satan to harass me, to keep me from becoming conceited. Three times I pleaded with the Lord about this, that it should leave me. But he said to me, "My grace is sufficient for you, for my power is made perfect in weakness." Therefore I will boast all the more gladly of my weaknesses, so that the power of Christ may rest upon me. For the sake of Christ, then, I am content with weaknesses, insults, hardships, persecutions, and calamities. For when I am weak, then I am strong. [5]

In this text, Paul is relaying a vision and how he could easily become self-confident based on what the Lord had shared with him in the vision. He experienced a realm of God that left him confident that Jesus is real. Based on his encounter with Him, He is assured of his assignment and that the power of Christ is resting upon him. He mentions a view of heaven, ecstasy and paradise. He is struggling to remain modest and not boastful. After all, it is difficulty to remain quiet about a real view of heaven… He now understands God's purpose for his life and declares that he has renewed spiritual strength, peace and joy. Therefore, Paul boasts of God's purpose for his Created Word. He notes that God's purpose will be accomplished and will prevail forever. God's purpose will not be stopped by humans, smashed by evil powers, or delayed by life's circumstances. Paul concludes by admitting that he had a medical condition, had asked Jesus to cure him, but instead Jesus' response was that His grace is sufficient because Paul's weakness would become strong for the Kingdom. The more he prayed and preached, the stronger he became for the glory of God. Paul did not die from his medical condition and he never ceased to pray. Like Paul, our infirmities make us strong in the Lord.

Review the steps of Prayer

1. Make a conscious decision that prayer is what you desire. Do you really desire to commit to prayer? What are you seeking through prayer?

2. Do you desire the things that are of the Lord? Are you prepared to seek Him for Christian things? Are you prepared to become a Christ-like follower?

3. Have you made a list of your desires, questions, or concerns related to prayer and commitment? If not, do so.

4. Locate and take advantage of a place for prayer. Look for a quiet place where your mind and thoughts are still. A place to concentrate on Jesus and prayer...

5. Prayer is talking with God. Talk and listen. Talk to Him as a wise and confident counselor. Listen to understand and recognize the voice of God.

6. Do not make idle or false promises to God. Remember the list? Write down your promises and make prayer a truth in your life.

7. Begin to love. Study love and what it means. Practice love every opportunity you get, no matter what. Relate your life and actions to love.

8. Praise and thank God for his revelation and responses to your prayer. (Remember, you know the voice of God).

9. Learning to commit and release your prayers to Jesus involves trust. When you trust your prayers to Jesus, you know longer continue to worry about outcomes.

10. Develop the practice of remaining with the Lord for worship. Worship in His Presence and He will reveal your gift, assignment and ministry call.

Changed Through Spiritual Warfare

Warfare involves conflict, competition and struggle between opposing forces that are out to silence you. It is usually one of several types of military operations between enemies. Warfare involves hostility, dislike, and a fight for territories. Warfare requires trained soldiers, skilled technicians, observant leaders and brave soldiers. The objective is to destroy or subdue the enemy before he does the same to your army. In this wise, spiritual warfare is a constant battle between the physical flesh and the Holy Spirit. It is a conflict between good and evil, fair and unfair, playing by the rule or making up the rule as you go, faith and faithfulness, Holy or unholy, or the believer and Satan. It is a never ending battle that endures for life. There is no set time or place for Spiritual Warfare. The enemy may be seen or unseen; the goal is to cause you to lose. It requires the whole armor of God to win. We are changed through Spiritual Warfare because we are trained, empowered and brave soldiers who are winners through the Blood of Jesus.

During the Biblical times, the influential and powerful did their business "in the gates." For example, the husband of the virtuous woman of Proverbs 31 is "known in the gates, when he sits among the elders of the land" (Prov. 31:23). Boaz, the intended husband of Ruth, went to the gate to buy a marriage license (Ruth 4:1–12; Deut. 25:7). War plans and military strategies were devised at the gate. Military treaties were signed at the gates (Judg. 5:8, 11). Kings sat in the gates to speak with their people (2 Sam. 19:8). Even conspirators against kings concocted their plots and were exposed in the gates (Esth. 2:19–23). In addition, the gate is used figuratively as a symbol of worship. Coming to worship is entering the gates (Psalm 24:7). The entrance to death is through the gate (Job 17:16). The entry to the heavenly city of God is spoken of as entering a gate (Rev. 21:12-15).

"So when Jesus spoke of the gates of Hades, He was drawing on a powerful image. Matthew's original readers would have seen it as a political metaphor, the way we use the terms City Hall, the White House, or the Capitol today. For them, the gates of Hades were not just a spiritual abstraction but actual forces of evil at work among human systems—the Roman government, for instance. While not evil in and of itself, first-century government was quickly becoming corrupted and also anti-Christian.

Jesus was alluding to a spiritual warfare of cosmic proportions. His followers are pitted against the powers of hell itself, which not only attack individual believers but seek to corrupt institutions, enlisting them in their campaign against Christ. Satan's guises can take many forms, as a look at any day's news will attest. Fortunately, Jesus also promised that in the end the gates of Hades would not succeed. That offers great hope to believers who live in difficult places and contend for good against powerful entities that, in ways known and unknown, are backed by spiritual forces of wickedness. In the midst of the fight Jesus has declared: "I will build my church!" Thus, spiritual warfare is the struggle between the forces of evil. It originated in the rebellion of Satan and his angels against God and how God has the final victory through Jesus Christ. Satan's desire is to use his army of well-organized angels of darkness who are seeking to persecute the church, oppose the gospel and attack individual believers. Believers are to fight with courage, determination, watchfulness, while standing in God's strength using the armor of God (Ephesians 6:11-20) and with prayer."[6]

Take the Territories

"Spiritual warfare is waged on three fronts: personal, corporate, and cosmic. In all three cases the war is waged against unseen enemies, principalities and powers, and evil in high places".[7]

Prayer strips the enemy of his powers and retrieves the territories he stole when one was distracted. A personal war is waged on families (husbands, wives, children and other relatives connected with the family). The enemy does not fight by the rules. He does not fight fair. When he is unable to win the head of the household, he begins a methodical tour of the family. Whether the process is corporate or cosmic, the process is halted through prayer which destroys his plans and resends the assignment back to the enemy.

Take Away Generational Curses and Familiar Spirits

Satan uses a force of demons (his co-workers) to carry out his plan of terrorism in the world. However, Jesus is the remover of curses and familiar spirits. He removes illness, disorders (mental or physical) and points humanity to Him as the only way out of our situations. The text points to conditions cured by Jesus as follows: Demon possession, deafness and muteness, paralysis and lameness, bleeding disorders, blindness and leprosy. Even death itself is cured by Jesus Christ through spiritual warfare prayer. Consequently, certain spirits that are familiar in the family line (for example) are prone to wreak havoc in that family. Asthma is a common bloodline disease that has a tendency to transfer from one family member to another throughout generations, *(2 Corinthians 10:4-5) For the weapons of our warfare are not carnal but mighty through God to the pulling down of strong-*

holds, casting down imaginations and every high thing that exalteth itself against the knowledge of God, and bringing into captivity every thought to the obedience of Christ;" (KJV)

Bind the Enemy and His Works

All human authority comes from God and it is to be used responsibly. Because all of our authority is given and established by God, we have the power to bind the enemy and his works through the Word, the Blood and the Name of Jesus. Please note that the ministry of deliverance is not for the unprepared, unsaved, or the faint hearted. It is a serious and powerful ministry that begins with worship and praise, centers on faith, thrives on the Biblical Text, discernment from the Spirit of God who determines the proper time as directed. The enemy is stripped of power by commanding the enemy and calling out every foul spirit of Satan you discern. We can command the spirit to leave without harming you or the person you are praying for without disturbance. Forbid him to re-enter the person. Ask the Holy Spirit to fill you or the person. Keep in mind, in order to defeat the enemy, Saints must use the warfare manual – God's Word, the Name of Jesus, and The blood of Jesus; and sleep in your armor. Please note some of **Satan's characteristics and strategies:**

Separate you from God	He is blind and will blind you	Satan is boastful and braggadocios	He plots against God's people	He is covetous of God's gifts to you
He is a fake and deceitful	He takes delight in your suffering	He is a destroyer of good things	He despises good and faithful work	He is disobedient and desires that you do the same
He uses evil to tempt and entice you	He is envious and jealous	He will lure you	He is foolish	Hard hearted and hateful
He is a liar	He is a hypocrite	He is a lover of pleasure (the world)	He is prayerless and hates the light of God	He is proud, stiff necked and selfish
He is unmerciful, ungodly, and unholy	He is sensual and unwise	He is a murderer and attempts to kill the Holy Spirit	He is unjust and unrighteous	He is not grateful, but he is a defeated foe…

Effective and Prevailing Prayer:
"Lord Teach Me How To Pray"
By Dr. Bertha Shavers - South Holland, IL

To understand effective and prevailing prayer, one must understand the definition of prayer. Here is one interpretation I have heard. "Prayer is an approach of our spirit by the power of the Holy Spirit helping us to stand before the throne of our Father." I like how Charles Spurgeon, in his book "The Power of Prayer in a believer's life", says it; "prayer is the spiritual transaction with the creator of *heaven and earth." It does not matter whether you are lying down, sitting up, on your knees, walking or in some cases while you are talking – you can reverence God by focusing on Him, the Giver of all things.*

As a child of God, I have come to share a few principles of prayer in order for each of us to become more prevailing and effective in our petitions to God. We all can be effective and powerful prayer warriors through the understanding that God requires us to have an active prayer life. 1 Sam. 12:23 says, Samuel would not sin against God for failing to pray for others. He understood the nature, significance and power of prayer.

Have you ever asked yourself, "What is prayer all about?" "Why are we called to pray?" The Holy Spirit is the one that grants us the power to be made effective prayer warriors? First: a sinner can pray and God will answer a sinner's prayers. The prayer must first be a prayer of repentance. But, for those who have already accepted God to be their Lord, he wants you to know that in order for you to be effective in your prayer life; you must know that praying or worshiping was ordained by Him. And, you are expected to enter into his presence.

There must be something to this thing called prayer because all the prophets of the Old Testament prayed;

- *Abraham prayed for Lot and his family; they were saved.*

- *Job prayed and stood firm in the midst of his trials.*

- *David prayed and changed God's heart toward the nation of Israel.*

Yes; there is something to this thing called prayer. Therefore, we can look to the scriptures and God's prophets for a clear perspective on how to pray effectively.

Prayer Was Ordained of God:

Throughout the Old Testament, God has instructed men through the simplicity of prayer. He has changed people and nations in his relationship with mankind. Psalm 50:15 says, "And call upon me in the day of trouble: I will deliver thee, and thou shall glorify me". We see that God wants mankind to communicate with Him and ask of Him what we need and he will answer our prayers. Today, prayer helps us to run the race of life. It also brings us into the inner strengths of God's purpose within our lives.

As the body of Christ, we view ourselves as two components of the body: soul and spirit. Our bodies have five senses; touch, taste, smell, sight and hearing – World-conscious. The soul/spirit is comprised of intelligence, will power, and emotions – Self-conscious. God is Spirit; and, we received our spirit from the breath of God. God says, "We are to worship Him in spirit and truth". Therefore, we can experience God through receiving the new birth with the in-filling of the Holy Spirit within our bodies (heart and spirit). The scriptures teaches that "we are to ask, seek and knock and the door will be opened".

Historically, God has made provisions for man to come before Him in thanksgiving, praise and worship. In the Old Testaments, God used the Tabernacle of Moses as the place where the people could come before Him and worship Him. Let's visualize this Tabernacle of Moses in order to better understand why God says we can approach Him through these same levels of thanksgiving, praise and worship.

For those who do not know what the Tabernacle of Moses is – I should give a little Jewish history here.

- *It was God's home on earth.*
- *He designed this so that his glory could dwell among men.*

- *He called Moses out from the people to set up a plan and pattern so that the people could come into his presence.*

- *It was a portable building that the Israelites carried throughout the wilderness.*

- *Men could not come anywhere near God's presence, because if they were to get too close to the presence of God, he (man) would be stuck dead.*

- *Men could only go into the outer court.*

- *Only the Priests were permitted within the Holy Place and every afternoon at precisely 3:00 in the afternoon, they went in to make the evening sacrifice.*

If you remember the Day that Christ died on the cross and gave up His ghost, it was also precisely at 3:00 in the afternoon. One could say that the priests watched as God rent the veil in two from the top to the bottom at precisely 3:00 when Jesus said, "It is finished".

The Outer Court:

The outer court represents thanksgiving, one of the three steps to approaching God for an effective and prevailing prayer. Enter God's outer court by way of thanksgiving (Ps 100:4). You must come before God to give Him thanks for what He has done for you in the past. This will build faith, and start your move toward the presence of God. A) At the Brazen Altar- (the Blood of Jesus), we deal with our sins and overcome our guilt by confessing our sins and experience God's forgiveness. B) at the Brazen Laver – (God's Word), we lay aside troubles, cares and fears by experiencing rest, relaxation, refreshing and renewal as we remember the Words of God. This is truly the place for each of us to wash ourselves of our personal sins before entering into a perfect God to learn how to pray.

The Holy Place - Learning How to Pray

This is the first tent like building in the outer court of the tabernacle. It represents praise. Praise God throughout the Holy Place (Ps 34:1). –It is where you begin to magnify God's character and praise him for His love, mercy, power, grace, longsuffering, and loving-kindness. Praise is not based on how you feel, but on your decision to bless the Lord at all times. A) The Table of showbread – (soul of man) submit your will to God and his plan. B) The Golden candlestick – (your mind) renew your mind according to the Word of God. Stop listening to what the world says and what your senses say, and start picking up what your spirit is saying. C) The Golden altar of incense – (submit your emotions) express your love to God. Let Him know that without Him you are nothing. Give Him all the praise. D) The Holy of Holies is the last room within the outer courts – this is the place where the presence of God dwelt. And freely enter the Holy of Holies with your worship- Here, only the priests would experience the presence of God. It contained the a) Ark of the Covenant – (sin is covered) and b) the mercy seat – (presence of God).

The Old Testament is only a pattern for the New Testament? (Heb 8:5, 6) *Hallelujah – Jesus the Christ went home and sent back the Comforter – The Holy Spirit. For us, God prepared something better than Moses' Tabernacle. We can now enter into God's presence with the power of the Holy Spirit.*

The Holy Spirit is our spiritual supplement. In that, He is the one that helps us to reach the Father. He will guide the believer into all things. As seen with the tabernacle of Moses, the Old Testament worshiper could only approach God through praise in the Outer Court and Holy Place. Only the priest had the duty and function of entering into God's Holy of Holies. The Word of God says that the Holy Spirit – Empowers the saints, glorifies Christ, and gives gifts to the church. He lives in the Believer, convicts us of sin, regenerates us, imparts God's love to us, gives us power, enables us to say "Jesus is Lord", helps us to pray, and has many other functions within the Believer's life.

But more importantly, the word of God says "that we must worship God in Spirit and Truth" this is the key to an effective prevailing prayer life, when one can enter the Holies of Holies in spirit and truth. One will get their prayers answered because God is not a man that He should lie. Another important point that should be noted here is the subject of speaking in tongues- the mysterious language that every believer receives from God. Matt. 6:6-13 basically says that our God is the subject of all our prayers. Praying in tongue is a necessary part of praying towards and worshiping the sovereign Father, in spirit, in truth and in faith. Praying in tongue is speaking to God. Always remember, both forms of prayer are acceptable to God.

What Does God Expect of us in Prayer?

God created man for one purpose – that is - to worship him. God's mercy just comes to some men. However, there are other mercies that are bestowed only upon those who ask and therefore receive; who seek; and therefore find; who knock; and therefore gain an entrance. So, there is a role for each of us to play in the art of prayer. Our role is to worship the Father in a relationship (through prayer). We must acknowledge God by giving Him the honor and reverence due Him. In James 5:16, the word says, "The effectual fervent prayer of the righteous man availeth much". This leaves me to feel that God wants us to be like Elijah – who was a righteous man that prayed earnestly that it might not rain; and it did not rain for three years and six months. Then he prayed again and it rained until the earth produced fruit. Although all can pray, one must have the empowerment of the Holy Ghost to have a powerful effective prayer life.

Jesus gave us the answer to how to have an effective prevailing prayer life in his response to his disciples when they said, "Master teach us how to pray". He gave them the Lord's Prayer found in the synoptic gospels. At that time, the Holy Spirit had not come. He is now in the earth and all believers have the ability to move into a powerful prayer life. My pastor has always told us "to pray through", do not stop when you feel a force coming against you; you are to press forward until you feel a release. This is prevailing in prayer. You may feel your nose running, your eyes watering and a heavy heart turning light allowing your sense to know that you have prevailed in prayer.

I conclude by saying we can now pray this powerful prayer outline or pattern that Jesus gave his disciples (below). And if you incorporate the visual of the seven pieces of furniture in the Tabernacle of Moses and read your Bible daily, you will have that effective prevailing power of the Holy Spirit helping you to enter into His Holy of Holies. Therefore, please have the following conversation with the Lord:

- *-**Our Father** – I am speaking to the Father of Creation; the Father of all mankind*

- *-**Who are in heaven** – Father you are enthroned and dwell in heaven, hearing my petition*

- *-**Hallowed be thy name** – Elohim (Plural of divine Persons), El-Elyon (The Most High God), El-Shaddai (God Almighty or All-Sufficient God), El-Olam (God, the Everlasting) and Jehovah (Yahweh, or Lord), Holy is your name.*

- *-**Thy kingdom come** – Lord allow your kingdom on earth as it is in heaven*

- *-**Thy will be done on earth as it is in heaven**- we have liberty, no illness and afflictions, nor lack or poverty and we are free of oppression here on earth as it is in heaven, I put you in remembrance of your words*

- *-**Give us this day our daily bread**- God our provider thank you for our daily bread and all our needs that are met daily*

- *-**As we forgive our debtors** – Father help me to forgive my debtors because I desire that you forgive me of my sins*

- *-**But deliver us from the evil one** – Please deliver us all from the evil one; allowing only your judgment to prevail over us.*

- *-**For yours is the kingdom and the power and the glory forever**- All things are yours and your kingdom is to come including all your power and glory forever Lord. Amen, Amen A-men. Speaking prayer in your life-style, Dr. Bertha Shavers.*

Assignment

Analyze the components of the prayer below and relate it to how you feel about God and yourself as follows:

Prayer Wisdom for the Lord's Prayer - Matthews 6:6-14 (KJV)

> [6] *But thou, when thou prayest, enter into thy closet, and when thou hast shut thy door, pray to thy Father which is in secret; and thy Father which seeth in secret shall reward thee openly.* [7] *But when ye pray, use not vain repetitions, as the heathen do: for they think that they shall be heard for their much speaking.* [8] *Be not ye therefore like unto them: for your Father knoweth what things ye have need of, before ye ask him.* [9] *After this manner therefore pray ye: Our Father which art in heaven, Hallowed be thy name.* [10] *Thy kingdom come. Thy will be done in earth, as it is in heaven.* [11] *Give us this day our daily bread.* [12] *And forgive us our debts, as we forgive our debtors.* [13] *And lead us not into temptation, but deliver us from evil: For thine is the kingdom, and the power, and the glory, forever. Amen.*

> [14] *For if ye forgive men their trespasses, your heavenly Father will also forgive you: (KJV)*

The Prayer explained (Matthews 6:6-14)

(1)   To whom to pray:

The Father, 6, 9.

(2)   Where to pray:

In the closet, alone with God, 6.

(3)   For what to pray:

The Father's glory, 9; the coming of His kingdom, the perfect doing of His will, 10; the   supplying of daily needs, 11; the forgiveness of sins, 12, 14; to be kept out of the place of temptation, deliverance from the evil one, 13; for everything we need, 8.

(4)   How to pray:

Reverently, 9; no unnecessary words, 7, 9–13; definite-

ly, putting God's glory first,   trustfully, 8, 9–13, to be heard of God and not to be seen of men, 6; with forgiveness to others, 12, 14; expectantly, 6, 9–13".[8]

Closing Prayer: *May we rejoice, become complete, be of good comfort, be of one mind, and live in peace; and the God of love and peace will be with us. May the grace of the Lord Jesus Christ and the love of God and the fellowship of the Holy Spirit be with us. (2 Corinthians 13:11, 14)*

Blessing and glory and wisdom and thanksgiving and honor and power and strength be to our God for ever and ever. Amen. (Revelation 7:12) May our Lord Jesus Christ Himself and God our Father, who has loved us and has given us eternal consolation and good hope by grace, comfort our hearts and strengthen us in every good work and word. (2 Thessalonians 2:16–17)[9]

3

Midnight: A Time of Great Darkness

Out of Your Control

(This was written while sitting in a hospital's waiting room, awaiting test results)

"Out of your control" is a true saying.
Many times, I've been repeatedly told;
But what can you do when things are spinning out of control?
This will happen when you set out to go beyond the preset mold;
You spin around, become dizzy and before you know it,
your life is out of control.
Satan will jump you, pluck you, shackle you,
and break you into pieces so small that you can't fold;
But, because God so loved the world, you can regain control
Compose yourself on your knees as a true saint,
praise, and worship like the saints of old;
You've got it, you can do it, take back your control
(R. Messenger, 1998)

Midnight: A Time of Great Darkness

From a family of eight children (Dorothy Spencer-Perkins (deceased), Lucas Lewis (deceased), John Lewis (deceased), (Lucas and John's father died when they were young), Leon Perry, (Pastor for over 21 years in Mississippi –deceased 2013), Bill Perry (Deacon and Trustee of our home church for many years – Mt. Salem M.B.C.), Rosie Perry-Messenger, Debra Perry-Parks, and Tempie Ann Perry-Morrow, we were born in an extremely rural area (if there is such area) in Tennessee, where poverty and desolation were the norms. Midnight was a time of great darkness. Mother had a fourth grade education, but she taught us about God, church etiquette, phonics, how to manage money, to respect ourselves and others, to cook, do laundry, the importance of education, and the mechanics of maintaining a CLEAN house (to name a few things). Mother often sat on the front porch at dusk, surrounded by the last three remaining younger girls at home and prayed that God would watch and keep her children and allow her to live to see them "grown" and doing well. The Lord honored her prayers. Even though, midnight has repeatedly struck the family, shaking its foundation, we have never ceased to pray. The following midnight situations, locations and people did not destroy our family structure:

- The oldest son (Lucas) died in a fire

- Mother had a Stroke in the car (with my brother Bill) on the way from church. It left her wheelchair bound. Two years later, the late night call came that mom had a few hours to live; she slipped away peacefully as my brother (Bill) and sister (Tempie) stood attentively by her bedside. During the entire process, they were in contact with the remaining siblings.

- A few years later, John died un-expectantly while hospitalized in Chicago; two or three years later, his wife Edna died.

- A few years later, Dorothy (the oldest girl) died at home with her family at her bedside

- Years past, and Leon's wife (Lois) died peacefully at home surrounded by the children; two or three years later, Leon became increasingly ill, unable to speak clearly, wheelchair bound, unable to eat, and had increasing trouble swallowing. He lost his battle in December, 2014. Midnight, AGAIN!

Although, we have experienced times of great darkness, we continue as a family, practicing what we were taught. We continued our relationship with Dad, Walter Jenkins, until he deceased. My siblings (Ann, Walter, James, William, Jeanette and Rayford) and a host of nieces, nephews and cousins are committed to prayer. We remember Mama and often laugh about funny things she said, her old-fashioned habits and especially her teachings. Because we continue to live and trust the same God that mom prayed to and talked about, we are united and well. We had to pray through our own midnight.

Real Life Midnight
Midnight Prayer from a Jailhouse (Acts 16:25-35)

"And at midnight Paul and Silas prayed, and sang praises unto God..." Acts 16:25 KJV). The prisoners heard them singing and praying and listened quietly. Ultimately, God sent an earthquake that shook open the jail cells that awakened the Guard. The prison guard woke up and did a bed check for escapees. But, all of the prisoners were accounted for. The narrative concludes with Paul and Silas ministering to the Guard and the prisoners. They went home with the Guard, ministered to his family, all were saved, and the magistrate ordered them released. Although, the jailhouse is a place of societal isolation with re-enforced walls of separation, Jesus is listening to jailhouse prayers. The jail cells have walls to separate one from their neighbor and the outside world. Security officers are posted in plain sight and surveillance cameras are mounted on every corner, wall and building. Imagine, how it feels to remain under observation twenty-four hours a day. Whatever one does, someone is watching. There is no privacy, comforts of home, no children and very little out-

side time. It is a place that one should not choose to live. Yet, there is comfort in knowing that God is available and willing to hear prayers of repentance, confession, and petition from a jail cell. Prayers from the inside of jail are continuing to reach the inside of heaven; the direct line to heaven intercepts the prayer and returns it to the prisoner who is praying with an answer. Satan attempts to hold up the prayer by a series of in-house crises, thus, creating constant midnight situations. Before one form of midnight has ended, another one is interjected. Instead of pressing, praising and praying through the existing midnight, satanic road blocks are implemented to cause doubt, fear and turmoil. During a midnight experience, the darkness plays mind games and Satan whispers that:

- "Things will be better during the day light, watch T.V. and do not worry about all that praying, this too will pass"

- "Call a male or female friend to make an emergency midnight visit – for conversation, after all, you are strong. Go ahead, you can handle it"

- "Turn on the radio for entertainment, this is old school, down home blues night. It will take our mind off your troubles and make you feel better".

- The negative self-talk replays over and over in your head. It is like pressing replay on the video

- Rehearsing how you will tell someone off – tomorrow will compound a midnight situation

- Scheming on how to obtain illegal things to make you feel better does not help

It is unwise to entertain the prior mentioned methods of solving or effectively dealing with your midnights. Think of ways to handle a lonely jail cell dilemma. Consider what it would (or will) take for you to legally leave and remain legally free. Prayer changes real life predicaments.

Midnight Darkness and Depression

Please note that the transition from midnight to the next day, only lasts one minute. When the clock strikes 12…, one minute later, it has passed midnight. The clinging and holding on to midnight issues simply prolongs the past negative experiences. When the church went into mass prayers for Peter (who was in jail), he appeared at the door before the prayer meeting had concluded. Prior to the saints storming heaven through prayer, he was asleep between soldiers, chained on both sides to another soldier. The angel awakened Peter and told him to arise, get dressed and put on his sandals. He led Peter to the closed and locked gate and the gate opened. Peter walked out and headed home, arrived and knocked on the door. A lady opened the door, thought she had seen a ghost, and closed the door in Peter's face. Peter simply knocked again and the door was opened. They were praying for Peter as he appeared at the door (Acts 12:5-19). Peter's midnight had passed. If you have been seeking God in prayer about matters from the heart, pray and listen for the knock. Often times it's the midnight that we are tuned into more so than listening.

Matthew 7:7 teaches that we should knock and ask and the door shall be opened to us. In this verse, Jesus is teaching his disciples atop a mountain. He spoke as the Son of God and addressed the law, anger, lust, divorce, retaliation, the needy, fasting, anxiety, and judging before chapter 7 begins. Chapter 7 picks up to address the concluding issue of judging, asking and forgiveness. Therefore, we have knocking authority that's recognized by the Son of God. He will hear and open the door in response to a sincere knock.

A midnight ministry is hands on ministry designed to combine and convey the knowledge of the gospel to others. The purpose of making and replicating disciples is to provide support through hard times, teach how to serve joyfully during darkness, and continue to pray throughout the midnight. People are important to someone who is experiencing depression "in the raw" at midnight.

Depression is alteration in the mental state noted by behavioral signs and/or symptoms of hopelessness, sadness, despair, discouragement, and discontentment. Also, there is noted a lack of desire to socialize (isolation), or fellowship. Severe depression may be characterized by hallucinations, stupor, or delusions. Depression may be situational in that it is activated by a stressful event, altered relationship issues, the environment, and a project that is not going as planned, or low self-esteem. It causes highs and lows in interactions. Like, Bi-po-

lar Disorder, it may consist of a mood disorder and depressive episodes

(including the highs and lows). However, similar to Diabetes, it is a

treatable condition. Until God delivers from depression, conversation,

prayer and "yes", even medication may be needed. Learn to celebrate

your midnight through prayer and well thought out treatments.

Midnight May Be a Time of Loneliness

With the Feeling of Abandonment

Webster explains loneliness as being without company, cut off from others, not frequented by human beings, desolate, sad from being alone, lonesome, a feeling of bleakness, or feeling alone. It means that the control or influence of another person or agent is given up with the intent of never again claiming certain rights or interests. It means (to withdraw from often in the face of danger) to withdraw protection, support, or help, to give (oneself) over unrestrainedly to cease from maintaining, practicing, or using. To cease intending or attempting to perform or interact with another. Abandonment leads to loneliness. Examples include, to desert, to forsake, or to leave without intention to return. It suggests that the thing or person left may be helpless without protection (like a child) and implies that the object left may be weakened but not destroyed by one's absence. (Webster electronic Dictionary)[1]

Youths and teenagers often experience loneliness, alienation

and the spirit of abandonment. "Did you know that?" The smallest

things may set off a trigger of past hurts and disappointment. It is im-

portant to pray them through their personal midnight journeys. Their

journey may stem from the diagnosis of mental or physical illness that

cause them to view themselves as "different" and "marred by the need for medication" to treat their illness. Grief is a major turning point for youths and teens who are un-churched or without the knowledge of Christ. It takes time to graciously lead them to saving grace and the understanding of separation through death. They are often teased for not wearing a particular brand of clothing, inability to afford the latest electronics, or not permitted to hang out and return home at any desired hour. Curfew is an old fashion word with "teens" and according to them, has no validity. They are often criticized for adhering to "house rules." We must pray and not permit degrading music, sordid movies and T.V. programs into the home. It is important to communicate with teens and teach them how to pray for themselves and others. Teens are toiling through midnight temptations and issues as follows:

- Tempted to <u>join in</u> the crowd (drink, smoke, use drugs, etc.)
- Tempted <u>not</u> to maintain celibacy
- Tempted to <u>disobey</u> parents or engage in gang or other <u>unlawful</u> activities
- Tempted to <u>abandon</u> Christianity, or become a bully
- Tempted to <u>drop out</u> of school and not pursue higher training/education
- Tempted to engage in <u>pre-marital sex</u> that presents huge midnight struggles
- Since babies are giving birth to babies, the tendency is to say, "<u>Pregnant</u> – now what"? The solution is to admit you have messed up, repent (become godly sorrowful), carry the baby to term, and explore the post-delivery options of adoption.
- Teased for <u>practicing abstinence</u> and engaging in healthy ac-

tivities

- Feeling lonely and abandoned, with <u>separation anxieties</u> from parents

Parents and guardians are responsible for noting and dealing with teens' temptations. Parents, "tune in to your teen through prayer."

Pressing Through the Darkness

You are not alone. You are not set apart to be picked apart. Yes, Satan is relentless and he does not play by the rules. However, he has "nothing new under the sun". He has no new tricks, but the same old ones. He specializes in catching you off guard. Stay awake and alert. For example, Satan constantly stood against the nation of Israel. He attacked Job and his friends because he hated Job's service to the Lord. He enticed Judas to betray Jesus (who was sinless). He has demonic messengers of darkness to harass the saints. He has many names: the devil, the serpent, the enemy, the adversary, etc. Peter invited him to get behind him. We may note that he is under our feet, a defeated foe, a loser, a trickster, a powerless snake, or a "pride filled fake". He is still defeated! Although he presents midnight in many forms, we are still winners through Christ:

- If you have ever had to wonder or did not know how you were going to pay the rent/mortgage, welcome to your midnight.
- If you have had to wonder whether or not your child was dead or alive in some faraway place, you have just experienced midnight.

- If you have ever had to fight your way out of your house to get to His House (church) only to find chaos in the church house and returned to violence back in your own house, you've been exposed to midnight dilemmas.

- If you are at the last extension on your unemployment benefits (with no other source of income), welcome to midnight…

It is during midnight that an emergency call is made to heaven for an expected day break solution. Break through at midnight. Challenge your midnight experiences with the Word. Seek advice, your midnight may be the result of poor and uninformed choices. You have heard the old saying, "If you can't beat them, join them." If you cannot overcome your midnights, welcome it and prayerfully celebrate it. Praise is a weapon of warfare that break yokes. In other words, wait for your midnight and take opportunity to praise God that you are still here to experience it. Hold on to the fact that you are still here to witness the nights melting into daylight. Find something to do. Witness as midnight creeps in and the quietness takes place. That is the time to begin to commune with God through the dark times.

Sing a song at midnight. It is not a time to spend time complaining about how bad you are feeling, when in essence, it is necessary to take time to know that you are saved. Christians are not exempt from suffering, sorrow, a few minutes of sadness or a time of regret. It is not what we go through, but it is how we go through. Realize that by serving the same Great God... His Promises are the same. Go ahead, you can do this! Began to tell God "thank you" for what He is to you. Tell Him, "thank you" for the things He has already done for you. Thank Him for what He has kept you from. Thank Him for where He is leading you during your time of adversity. Pray and press through the dark times.

Walking Thru Midnight With a Prayerful Attitude
By
Pastor Herbert Lee, Jr.,
Sr. Pastor of New Progressive Baptist Church; Chicago, IL
(Married to Naomi Tobias-Lee)

Midnight is the transition time period from one <u>day</u> to the next: It is the moment the date changes. In the <u>Roman time system</u>, midnight was halfway between <u>sunset</u> and <u>sunrise</u>, varying according to the <u>seasons</u>. (Wikipedia) A deep or extended darkness or gloom. (Merriam Webster) The Bible recorded several events that happened at midnight.

> • In Exodus 11:4:6, the Lord said to Moses, "About midnight will I go out into the midst of Egypt: [5] And all the firstborn in the land of Egypt shall die, from the firstborn of Pharaoh that sitteth upon his throne, even unto the firstborn of the maidservant that *is* behind the mill; and all the firstborn of beasts.[6] And there shall be a great cry throughout all the land of Egypt, such as there was none like it, nor shall be like it any more.

> • In Acts 16:25, Paul and Silas were in jail in Philippi, and at midnight Paul and Silas prayed, and sang praises unto God: and the prisoners heard them.

Midnight, as it relates to time is the halfway point or the dividing line between what was and what will be. But figuratively, it speaks of a time of trouble or some difficulty in one's life. For us, Midnight will certainly come. It may be sickness, the death of a loved one, a financial crisis, or some other form of devastation, but midnight will come. The time will come to a believer in Christ (Christian), or a non- believer (non-Christian). However, the difference is how we respond to our midnight. Paul and Silas are good examples for us to follow when we are facing our midnight.

Paul had a vision and saw a man from Macedonia requesting that he come to Macedonia and help them. This vision led him to believe that the Lord Jesus Christ was calling him and Silas to preach the gospel in Macedonia. (Acts16:9) It was there in Philippi that they were placed in jail for casting the spirit of divination out of a girl. These men did not complain about their midnight situation. Instead, they prayed and sang praises to God.

Yes, Midnight will come, but we don't know when. As Christians, we can be certain that God knows the exact time. Since He knows all things, we need to go to Him with a prayerful attitude and ask, "Lord, what are you trying to teach me? Will this bring glory and honor to you? Then we need to pray, not my will but thy will be done.

Amen – Blessing to you as you travel beyond your midnight. Pastor Lee.

Assignment

1. Share a time you experienced great midnight darkness in your life and the steps you had to take to manage the situation.

2. How would you minister to a person in jail on false charges?

4

A Call to Holiness
(1 Peter 1:13-16)

A Dollar and a Penny

A dollar and a penny, a little, that can help many.

The two are always at church and shows up in the offering plate; oh that dollar and a penny.

"Lord, I wish I could do better, but you know I have to pay the rent by Monday or it will be late.

Lord, you know my heart and what I desire for your kingdom cause; but that's all I had left, and I put it all in the offering plate.

You see, Jesus, I have to pay the car note and keep car fare for tomorrow. My boss is already on my back. Next week, I will make up for the slack

Now understand, I will eventually pay you your ten percent, but, you did give me wisdom and five senses.

When the trump sounds, the cloud splits and the Master appears, keep your money in your pocket and your excuses in your mind. It will be too late to pay up by that time.

Face it! You've turned your own sword inward, now you are falling dead to your own financial spear. No need to make excuses now, the end is near. You will face the dreaded fear of many.

Because you have become prey to the dollar and the penny?

(By R. Messenger, 1996)

A Call to Holiness (I Peter 1:13-16)

I Peter 1:13-16 teaches that we are "called to be holy". Holiness is our life (future and present), and we should spend it separating ourselves from worldly practices. Holiness is our aspiration to align ourselves with Christ and his redemptive work. So, "What does it mean to be a holy person?" The correct response should be that you are attempting to be like Jesus. Are you? Are you free from the practice of sin? Are you in a healthy focused state in Christ? What about your state of mind? Are your desires healthy? How far does your holiness go…? Does it stop, once you have exited the church building, or does it carry over to your home, work, and outside activities? Do you have a secret life that you pray no one ever discovers? If not, prepare yourself to be set apart from the world and unto Christ Jesus. God's holiness ushers in pure thoughts, ministry works, and the manifestation of spiritual gifts, prayer, praise and worship. God honors moral excellence through Him. Remember, "Saints are called to be holy because the God they serve is holy."

God's holiness is matchless. His very name is Holy! His abode is holy. We worship him in holiness and truth. We look to him for peace, mercy, joy, restoration, forgiveness and comfort. If God is love that means His holiness is love. Thus Peter writes:

> [13] *Therefore, preparing your minds for action, and being sober-minded, set your hope fully on the grace that will be*

brought to you at the revelation of Jesus Christ. [14] As obedient children, do not be conformed to the passions of your former ignorance, [15] but as he who called you is holy, you also be holy in all your conduct, [16] since it is written, "You shall be holy, for I am holy." [17] And if you call on him as Father who judges impartially according to each one's deeds, conduct yourselves with fear throughout the time of your exile, [18] knowing that you were ransomed from the futile ways inherited from your forefathers, not with perishable things such as silver or gold, [19] but with the precious blood of Christ, like that of a lamb without blemish or spot. [20] He was foreknown before the foundation of the world but was made manifest in the last times for the sake of you [21] who through him are believers in God, who raised him from the dead and gave him glory, so that your faith and hope are in God. [22] Having purified your souls by your obedience to the truth for a sincere brotherly love, love one another earnestly from a pure heart, [23] since you have been born again, not of perishable seed but of imperishable, through the living and abiding word of God; [24] for "All flesh is like grass and all its glory like the flower of grass. The grass withers, and the flower falls, 25 but the word of the Lord remains forever." And this word is the good news that was preached to you. I Peter 1: 13-16 (ESV)

The text declares that God's love for us is like a parent and a child's image of love and relationship. We are to remain thirsty for the knowledge of God and prepared to act on His behalf at all times. As we love, honor and obey our parents, so we teach our children to do likewise and so we display the same attitude, demeanor, trust, and obedience to God. He has left His Word for our learning and He has modeled perfect behavior as our example. What other model do we need? We need to practice what we have been taught, what we have studied, what we have learned and what the Holy Spirit has revealed to us through the Word, prayer, praise and worship. Holy folk obey God.

He has declared us citizens through Calvary. Once we are saved, we are to prepare and continue a life of holy living.

Prepare Your Mind for Living Holy…How?

Holiness and holy living are not based on a designated area or place. Yet, it is a suit that should be worn for the duration of "our" lives. Please note that holiness is not grounded in a building or a denomination, but on Jesus and His redemptive work for us. So, it is a way of life committed to imitating the life of Jesus. Holiness says, "We are models for Christianity. We are modeling His character, displaying His behaviors and living out our salvation based on obedience to the Biblical text. The Text provides guidelines on how to prepare and live holy. The Holy Text provides Christ's keys to the practice of holy living because,

"Christ has already invited us into the most holy place there is, so that we will live as His holy people in everything we do (Heb. 9:11–15; 10:19–25)".[1]

Holiness is non-violent, peaceful and serene living in synchronization with Jesus and others through the Word. Holiness is honesty and integrity. It is Christian standards rooted in Christ-centered trustworthiness and devotion to ministry. Holiness exemplifies Kingdom living and kingdom upkeep through prayer, praise, worship, tithes and offerings. Holy folk share tithes and liberal offerings! How do you prepare for holy living? The preparation begins with a thirst for righteousness. The thirst carries over to a careful study of the Word illuminated by sound doctrinal teaching (not denominational teaching, but Biblical teaching). The process penetrates the mind and changes the heart. Armed with Christ's mind, new areas are awakened for the homeless and others who are experiencing a life of midnights and yourself via a steady diet of "rightly divided" teachings; holiness is considerate, patient, generous and modestly attired. In holiness, Christ is first. What happens when you put God first? Work through the prep work by separating yourself, ways, behavior, and commitment and ministry involvement unto Christ. When we practice sanctification and righteous living... *"we have great cause to praise and thank the Lord as we read Leviticus. Here we have a picture of what it cost Jesus to make us right with God. We also have a picture of what our response should be—a life of holiness".* [2]

How to Prepare Your Mind for Holy Living:

- Receive and accept Jesus as your personal Savior

- Make a conscious decision to diminish the negative people, places and things in your life by aligning them with God's Word;

- Seek to imitate godly behavior through weekly Bible study, regular intercessory prayer, Sunday school attendance, connection with the men and women's ministries, and other forms of Christian teachings and discipleship training. Skip the secular stuff!

- Change the way you do things and become more mindful of the company you are keeping on a regular basis; Garbage in, garbage out.

- Keep your physical temple (body) holy and refrain from pre-marital and extramarital indulgences. Change your crowd. Live for the Lord.

- Study Christ's example from the gospels (Matthew, Mark, Luke and John). Learn of Him.

- Dismiss arrogance, boasting, conceit, fear and especially pride. These behaviors often are carnal replacement for what a person does not know or something they are seeking to cover. Your salary is of little interest when it comes to where you will spend eternity.

- Reassess yourself often and make modifications as needed for growth

Ground Your Hope in Holiness

Dig in and develop roots in holiness. Trust is a giant step. Start with small steps (if needed) and become a person that God can trust with His Word and His people. Abuse of power is a serious infraction of who God desires us to be. You must be trustworthy in the midst and around God's people. Permit His Word to motivate your life. Above all, permit trouble, odd situations, valleys and trenches to shape your Christian life. (Note: Christians are not exempt from trouble). Allow hope and holiness to marry and form a bond of trust in you. The ulti-mate belief is that one day you will enter into God's eternal rest. Holi-ness speaks to separation unto God. Hope is expecting to, but reigning is being with... Him forever. Because of our hope in Christ, we are assured that He will reward our service with eternal and everlasting life. Holiness teaches us to live in anticipation of receiving something at the end of our earthly life.

Holiness is a thought changer, but hope brings our thoughts into change. God commanded holiness through the Word, but hope is the desire to live out the Word. We are inspired to live and become a sinless perfection (which is impossible in this life), but we are to continue to reach for it. Our hope in Jesus serves to illuminate and remind us of what the heart meant to do to help us to continue to live in holiness. His holiness warns, rebukes and tests us, but His hope places a bandage on our sore spots and desires to soothe and remind us that God still loves us, no matter what we have done. Thus, holiness is changing our practice from sin to righteousness so we may have favor with God. In hope, we expect to see God as shown in I Corinthians and in John which,

...gives a fourth motive for dedicated living: the price Christ paid on the cross. Before we were saved, our lives were empty and meaningless ("vain"—v. 18); but now they are full and happy through Him. Our salvation was not purchased with money; it took the blood of Jesus Christ, the spotless Lamb of God (John 1:29). His death was planned by God ages before we ever were born; yet, God in His grace included us in that plan! How grateful we should be, and what better way is there for us to show our gratitude than to surrender our all to Him (1 Cor. 6:15–21).[3]

Holiness is the responsibility of every Christian. Like an athlete training for the Olympics, there must be a commitment to become physically fit, practice healthy eating habits from the fruit of the Spirit, and a regime of long hours of exercise. Holiness is what helps us to "Run", but hope is what keeps us running and focused on the prize." Pray without ceasing, and know the Word of God is God's formula for winning races.

Conform to Christ-Centered Living

What is Christ-centered living? It is simply a life centered on biblical teachings and based on a belief in the Gospel story of Jesus Christ as Lord. The ultimate goal is to "be like Him" in all that we say, do, teach, practice and preach based on the Biblical text. Therefore, our lives become centered on the things for, about and related to Christ and His Redemption. Thus, we (saints) emulate His sinless life, His patient suffering, His meek demeanor, and His persistence for our right to live. For example, living for Christ means a life dedicated to "favoring Him". We have to mind how we live and conduct our daily affairs for the rest of our lives. That means marriage is of God and "living together", "civil unions", "same-sex marriages," or "shacking up" are not of God and not Christ-Centered because:

According to a report from Family Scholars on "Why Marriage Matters, Third Edition (Thirty Conclusions from the Social Sciences) there are thirty conclusions related to the family, economics, physical health and longevity, mental health and emotional well-being, and crime and domestic violence. This writer will present only the excerpt from the fundamental conclusions of the family structure and process as follows:

1. *Marriage increases the likelihood that fathers and mothers have good relationships with their children*

2. *Children are most likely to enjoy family stability when they are born into a married family.*

3. *Children are less likely to thrive in complex households*

4. *Cohabitation is not the functional equivalent of marriage*

5. *Growing up outside an intact marriage (between a biological male and female)increases the likelihood that children will themselves divorce or become unwed parents*

6. *Marriage is a virtually universal human institution.*

7. *Marriage, and a normative commitment to marriage, foster high quality relationships between adults, as well as between parents and children*

8. *Marriage has important biosocial consequences for adults and children* [4]

The prior eight conclusions are evidence that living a Christ-centered life involves every component of life, especially the family structure.

Understand the Call to Live Holy

Remember, like salvation, holiness is a choice. It is up to you to make the choice of whether or not you will accept God's salvation plan for your life or not. To this end, we are to understand that God is holy and not malicious. We must pattern our lives after his attributes. In addition, He is the measurement for our lives. When we learn, develop and practice the standards he has displayed for us, we will live in agreement with each other through His holiness. It takes a prayerful understanding to actively engage ourselves in a holy walk.

As previously stated, "God is holy and righteous". Righteous is "acting in accord with divine or moral law" (Merriam-Webster Dictionary). It is freedom from the price for practicing sin. It involves morals, scruples, faith, and justification. A righteous mind makes righteous decisions, but a mind centered on prejudice outrage and injustice will produce immoral decisions that results in sin. Sin and ungodliness should displease God's people. In that vein, evangelism is important. It should begin in the household of faith and spread outward to the world. It is imperative that we practice righteous behaviors. Saints are not to engage in secular activities, immoral conduct, and the known practice of sin. Why? Because sin is missing the mark! The remedy is regular Bible study attendance, Sunday school involvement, attending small group meetings and classes and daily intercessory prayer ministry engagement to become and replicate discipleship.

Because God is the epitome of righteousness, self-righteousness is man's way in the flesh. Flesh and blood will not please God.

The self-righteous person has tunnel vision, immoral practices, and a prideful spirit and disregards God's instructions for holiness. If the shoe fits you, do not wear it, but take this time to check your life and repent. Next, accept Christ's salvific plan for you and ask Him to become the head of your life. Then reflect back and begin to praise God for keeping you in-spite of you. Allow your praise to flow into worship. Worship will get you there, right into His presence… Press until you have entered the spiritual realm. It is in the spiritual realm that God will show you yourself, how to live, areas of needed improvement, and other areas that He desires to spiritually mature you. Righteousness speaks to God's character and how He deals with man. God is not a respecter of persons. You are overdue for your new assignment.

Romans 3:21-26 teaches that God is a Savior to sinners. He died to pay the cost for wrong because no other human had been able to do so. Of course, He sent king after king, the prophets, apostles, bishops, armies and captors, but they all came short and had no ability to keep themselves apart from God. Jesus came in perfect righteousness. He is returning to judge the world in righteousness. Jesus never compromised His call, His mission, His holiness, His death, His burial or His resurrection. We are not to compromise His gospel.

Conduct Yourself as Becoming Holiness

In order to live holy, it is vital to "walk in the light" of God. Pretentious holiness is temporal and short-lived, at best. Various forms of holiness are practiced to give the illusion of holy living. Examples include, but are not limited to:

- A strict regime of only one type of apparel that covers up everything but the eyelids.

- The practice of not wearing a tasteful and practical application of make-up

- The practice of not wearing simple and modest jewelry

- The "never watch T.V." type of holiness

- The "beat down" type of evangelism to the public

- The public ridicule of other denominations, and the list goes on

However, if this serves to keep you grounded in your faith, by all means practice it in combination with rightly dividing the Word of Truth and the practice of modesty in all you do. The goal is not to permit traditions or rituals to hinder your growth toward righteous and holy living. After all, holy conduct must demonstrate an understanding of holiness and its requirements. Otherwise, you have severed yourself from Christian teachings. A member of a clique instead of a Holy Ghost filled ministry is not authentic holiness. Do not underestimate temptation. It is endlessly before the saints. That is the importance of following a leader who is rooted and grounded in the "True-Vine." Real leaders are connected. Their leaders are connected to Jesus. Thus, there is a formation of Spirit-filled leaders and followers. That pleases Jesus. That is a win-win follow-ship, consistent with you becoming holy and maintaining a life of holiness.

Encouragement to Embrace Holiness From a Teenager's Perspective (18 years old)

The Question:

To what extent can a gay teenager develop a plan for peace while using Facebook from 3:00pm until 11:00pm?

By

Amina L. James,

YAT (Youth and Teen) Ministry of

Holy Rock Church & Outreach Ministries, Chicago, IL

As a high school teenager, my concern for peace reaches out to my peers who experience harassment and discrimination on social media. One of the world's largest causes of cyber bullying is developed from gay teenagers being picked on from generally the ages 11-18 due to their choice of sexuality. Cyber bullying has been a way of attacking teenagers since its beginning. Many students have been attacked using electronic distribution of photos, advertisement of private information and being participants of viewing cruel online posts toward each other. Many gay people have become victims of discriminatory language, which has been designed to humiliate gay teenagers by including terms like that's so "gay", "fag", and by simply saying, "you gay". The terms have been used to show the difference in the character of a person. A person can destroy the self-esteem and self-confidence of other individuals when they brag about how they have become unpopular from the regular society that is classified as a, "world filled with heterosexuals". This is one reason why twenty-eight percent of gay students will drop out of school. This is more than three times the national average for heterosexual students. (Bart, M). The world has been created in which we are all equal but have different beliefs and morals of how we feel individuals should live their lives. We can agree to disagree   with our brothers' beliefs. What I mean by agree to disagree is that we don't have to practice someone else's beliefs, but we should respect their principles. Laws are created to protect the rights of gay individuals, but there still has not been a decrease in the amount of harassment they encounter. It has been discussed that there should be laws that promote nondiscrimination and a right to choose their sexuality at their own desire. This has been implemented in most places around the world but, not practiced by all. Although the laws have been created, people don't follow them. So, gay individuals are still a popular outcast in today's society.

Facebook

Facebook has been acknowledged to be ranked the world's number one site of social network. Anyone can have free access to this site, if they apply. The social network Facebook has been created to give individual citizens the opportunity to share and connect with other people, whether it's family, businesses, or just to chat with new people (Mark Zuckerberg/Facebook). By joining Facebook, people have the right to share whatever information they want and can connect online with anyone, organization or service but both must agree to the connection of one another (Facebook). Facebook gives people the opportunity to take ownership of their own information. They have freedom to decide with whom they will share their information, and to set privacy controls to protect those choices. However, the control buttons are not totally responsible for how people receive and accept the posted blogs that can be viewed worldwide (Facebook). Most importantly, Facebook has been established to send geographic and national boundaries and is available to everyone in the world with no applying restrictions (Facebook). Although Facebook has been used for negative aspects, like harassment, it has also been used in the positive area as well. People have reunited with family and friends while using Facebook. Facebook has allowed some people to advertise. Facebook has allowed people to promote their organization and business.

Facebook is not only a negative site, but it is and can be an edifying site for the good as well. Facebook is where a person can try and promote a peaceful and caring world. Facebook can pertain to teenagers because it's a site that is used more often by them than the older generation. Initially, Facebook was a site designed to give people an opportunity to reunite or stay in contact with their classmates from previous classes. It allowed them to keep in contact with their teachers because they could inbox them or even find them just to keep in contact. Facebook is effected by different regions because each region has their own rules and levels of tolerance. The United States is a place of freedom and is not as strict as other regions may be. Each region has different expectations and exposure to Facebook. Their level of harassment might differ due to the size of population and the events that occur within their region.

Harassment and Its Connection to Facebook

However, as a witness, Facebook does not achieve these goals because society has remodeled it to fit their living purposes, which is causing damage to the teenage generation. It has been modified from its original purpose of why it was designed. People have turned Facebook into a gossip session and a place to vent their thoughts. Facebook users are destroying the lives of gay teenagers every day. They feel useless to society because they are looked upon as being different and not living up to who everyone else's expectations of them. Facebook can be used to benefit the world. But in most cases, it has been used in the negative way which is to destroy children and teenagers' minds. Posting negative pictures, making negative rumors, cracking jokes, and sending bashful messages worldwide through Facebook can influence the feelings of a gay teenager and how they feel and connect to society and how society accepts them and their living status of life. Although Facebook introduces their Terms and Conditions, all Facebook users need to be cautious of the pictures they upload and the comments they make because of the effect it has on gay people. GLBT students are more apt to skip school due to the fear, threats, and property vandalism directed at them (Garofalo, R. Wolf, R.C., Kessel,

S., Palfrey. J). One survey revealed that 22 percent of gay respondents had skipped school in the past month because they felt unsafe there (Chase, Anthony).

Online jokes, insults, rumors, pictures or videos can also impact an individual's reputation and their employment and learning opportunities. This allows everyone to see what he or she is involved in. Jokes can ruin the person's reputation because depending on how funny the joke is there will be many followers, who like the post. These things cause a person to lose their dignity. Cyber bullying can negatively impact an individual's health and well-being. Cyber bullying can leave a person traumatized and cause them to feel insecure. They will begin to feel that they are not worth anything and they do not fit in. These types of feelings can cause a person to become depressed and stressed. Harassment can decrease a student's performance at school because they become so distracted and embarrassed that they feel they need to drop out of school or move to a different school as a result of feeling left out of their school environment. One of the most devastating aspects of harassment and cyber bullying is suicide. Gay teens in U.S. schools are often subjected to such intense bullying that they're unable to receive an adequate education (Chase, Anthony.) They're often embarrassed or ashamed of being targeted and may not report the abuse.

Although Facebook is a site used more commonly by teenagers, I believe parents play a part in gay harassment. Gay youths feel they have nowhere to turn. According to several surveys, four out of five gay and lesbian students say, "they don't know one supportive adult at school". Parents play a part in this manor because as adults, if they hear or view someone being harassed, they should take leadership and report it whether they know the person, child or student or not. They should feel enough sympathy as adults to stand against the bullies and tell them they will show some concern about ending cyber bullying of gay harassment. I feel that parents should be mandated reporters because they understand how the teenagers are dealing with these situations. The bullied person could be too afraid to speak up for themselves, but if the adults would do it, they would feel that they have someone to turn to when they feel alone. Parents play a part in the cyber bullying harassment because they do not monitor their child's activities on the internet. Although I know most parents feel that they can trust their child enough to give them privacy, they should still be cautious of the things their children are exposed to. Parents can make a difference because they are the ones that are responsible for the behavior of the child that's being harassed in which they can have an input, and they also are responsible for the bully, in which they can monitor the things they post and their comments.

Facebook leaves their users with the feeling of lack of privacy and lack of social responsibility that often develops from using online communications, and many students post embarrassing, humiliating and hurtful content in text, photos and videos. Nothing is private on-line, especially on the online social networks. Serious consequences have occurred to those who have been a part of an online behavior problem when it is made public. Students can be expelled from school. Students' families can be sued for slander and harassment. Most importantly, a student can be arrested for violating the right of a gay individual.

Statistic for Harassment

Statically, harassment has been the biggest cause of incidents among the teenage generation. There have been suicide deaths, school drop outs, stress claims and health issues. According to recent gay bullying statistics, gay teens are two to three times more likely to commit teen suicide than other youths (Bullying Statistics). According to statistics, nearly 30 percent of all completed suicides have been related to sexual identity crisis (Bullying Statistics). Students who also fall into the gay identity groups over decades report being five times more likely to miss school because they feel unsafe after being bullied due to their sexual orientation (Bullying Statistics). About 28 percent of those groups feel forced to drop out of school because they have become so over whelmed by the stress of being gay. (Bullying Statis-

tics). Although more and more people are working to end or fix the problems with bullying, teens are still continuing to bully each other due to sexual orientation and other factors (Bullying Statistics). This is a factor that is never expected to end. Studies show that young people are more exposed to this life style than an older person would be. (Bullying Statistics).

In a 2005 survey about gay bullying statistics, teens reported that two reasons they are bullied is because of their sexual orientation or gender choice (Bullying Statistics). The number one reason reported was because of appearance (Bullying Statistics). The word teenager means a young adult is mentally growing. They are in their young adult lives in which they are trying to find out how they play a part in society. They are more concerned about how they fit in than how they can make a difference in life. As they grow and mature, they begin to wonder what it takes to become similar to their peers. Young teenagers are more consumed with what their friends would think of them than making a wise decision that will benefit them in the future. So therefore statistics have shown how being teased, bullied and harassed is something that will negatively affect a person's self-esteem and how they will view themselves even through their adulthood.

Generally 5 out of 10 gay teens have reported being bullied within the past year because of their sexual desire according to the most recent gay bullying statistics (Bullying Statistics). Out of the 5 of 10 numbers, almost half have reported being physically harassed or followed by another and a quarter who reported actually being physically assaulted (Bullying Statistics). According to recent statistics, out of the students that did report harassment or bullying situation, the trusted adult did not react to the situation, so the child withdrew and acted upon it themselves (Bullying Statistics). The case of gay harassment is still on the rise. There have not been enough consequences reported to make the number of statistics decrease. The number of gay harassment incidents must not continue to rise but shall be decreased through prayer. . What will it take to change the Facebook and other forms of harassments? It will take prayer to bring peace.

Pray, Plan, Peace

In conclusion, as a witness of social media exposure, there are many things that can be modified to make the social media a more peaceful site. In order to set one's self free from being humiliated, we must pray, develop a plan, then we will be able to have peace. While in the process of gaining peace we must remember that the race is not given to the swift, nor to the strong, but to those who endure through the hardship of the race. In order for a person to feel that they are at peace with the world, they must accept themselves and pray that God gives them a clean heart. They should seek God for answers about their true identity and ask the question, "God, did you make a mistake?" When they identify themselves, then they can understand why they are different, living in the world. We must pray for and with those who are willing to hear and accept Jesus Christ as their Savior.

We must clarify and witness to those who don't seem to get the point about the choices that they make. One thing bullies must come to realize is, when you post something that humiliates a person's dignity, you cannot restore the loss, but God can. Although that person may feel helpless, they can develop a plan for peace by speaking against bullying and reporting to their parents, ministers, pastors, relatives or any trusted adult the issues they are experiencing. First step to developing a plan for peace is accepting who you are even when peers don't. This means acknowledging the fact that they are different but unique contributors to other people who love them and are praying for them. This can help them to gain peace within that group (Christians and other fellowship social groups) so that they will realize that someone supports them and that they are important to someone else, especially God. Within this fellowship, they will learn to cope with the situation and understand the mentality of a bully. Bullies have major issues. Therefore, they will have fewer burdens because they don't have to deal with them alone. A gay teenager can develop a plan of peace by praying against demonic spirits of homosexuality. The prayers are where they will begin to learn their identity and gain confidence in the person they are, if they become convicted that they are not following God's commandments for His people. Prayers will promote anti-bullying and will cause people to gain self-confidence, if they become sincere. Most importantly, they will develop a plan for peace by taking their weaknesses and turning them into positive actions so that society will no longer tend to single them out. Remember, prayer changes, people, locations and things in our lives. Bless you, Amina.

Assignment

How are you living? Please review the below listed information and check all that apply to your current state of holiness. This is a learning tool! Please check what you consider holy or unholy by placing an "H" for holy and a "U" for unholy.

Is it holy, or unholy?

_ A strong drink once a day
_ Prefers secular music when driving alone
_ An occasional flare up of a foul word
_ Unable to forgive related to a childhood incident; or other offenses
_ Unable to practice an even temperament
_ Cannot afford to pay tithes or give a liberal offering
_ Unable to rid self of "a jealous" spirit
_ Have my own ministry outside (independent) of my church's ministry
_ Often stay home and watch T.V. church. It's the same thing anyway
_ Go to a steppers set or to the club weekly to every other week. "I can still witness there"
_ When others do not praise my "good works", I perceive that they are jealous and/or intimidated by me
_ No one can tell me how to dress. "After all, I am grown and can see how I look, myself"
_ I have lied, does that mean I am unholy?
_ I am compelled to lie to make myself look good before others. It is no problem, I just want to make myself feel important and knowledgeable. Am I holy?

"Search me, O God, and know my heart; test me and know my anxious thoughts. See if there is any offensive ways in me, and lead me in the way everlasting (Psalm 139:23, 24). KJV

5

Prayer Stirs People

Throughout the progression of time, prayer has caused an upheaval in the lives of God's people. The secular world turns to prayer in times of uncertainty and discontent and that is a good thing to do. Society and the world at-large are aware of the need to communicate to a "Higher Power" that is in control of the universe. Yet, when all is going well, their prayers are silent. For example, Rock Stars, Pop Singers, R&B singers, and especially Rap Stars are noted to wear the crucifix; some with Jesus still on the cross, others with Jesus off the cross. At the onset or following a vigorous round of vulgar acts and embarrassing lyrics on stage, a higher power is recognized. During times of devastation, the request goes out over the airways and social media to pray for those in crisis and that is a good thing. But what about a life that is stirred to change though prayer?

On 9/11, the nation stood by and remained vigilant in prayer following the collapse of the "Twin Towers". But before the Towers had fallen or before their request went out, the saints all over the world were praying. Every nation, language, nationality, race, creed, and color were praying for comfort, peace, and the capture of those who were responsible for the grotesque act. The President quoted from the Biblical text and requested that the United States pray for safety and peace. Can you, the reader, believe that God had already pre-destined or pre-determined who would escape the horrific and cannibalistic act? Yet, it was by His mercy and grace that others are alive with their testimonies. He allowed us to learn from the travesty so that we are able to know and trust Him. New coping strategies were developed that included God through an unfortunate incident. Victims and their families continue to pray and depend on Him for their recovery. Why? Because God stirred the people to pray through calamity. He is continuing to comfort and stir people that would have never known about ministering to the physical and spiritual in ministry positions. For others, God is bringing them to the end of their midnight, and they are viewing the light at the end of the tunnel. Man must learn how to pray because prayer stirs the lives of people.

Learn How to Pray

Again, review Dr. Shavers' segment on "Lord Teach me How

to Pray" in Chapter 2. Begin to practice the lesson. It is one thing to read the instructions, but it is different when the instructions are implemented. In other words, it takes practice to perform the task. Perhaps you are not comfortable with praying in public. That is alright. Learning to pray will become a practice and a duty, if persistence is maintained.

It is good to pray always. Start your day with prayer. Do not be afraid to ask the Almighty Son of God to "Teach me how to pray". After all, He is prayer. Jesus prayed to His Father (God) throughout the Biblical text. He took time to pray with and for others, and He taught His disciples to pray. Paul admonishes us to pray without ceasing.

- Begin by speaking to Him, "Good morning Holy Spirit", "Jesus, it's me", or "Lord, I am experiencing tough times and I need your help" and proceed from there. It is not like He does not already know your dilemma. He wants you to not only know your dilemma, but to include Him in it.

- The next step is to empty out on Him. Talk with Him about your true feelings of hurt, rejection, low-self-esteem, inadequacies, etc. Acknowledge that you have heard about Him and that you have discovered that He is the God of your saved ancestors, now you are open to His **salvific** plan for your life.

- Next, be honest. Acknowledge your short comings and repent of things that may hinder your prayer. Thank Him for past and present blessings. Ask Him to allow you to enter His presence (the spiritual realm).

- Listen for His still, small voice that is saturated with LOVE. Remain there as you worship Him for who He is.

- Listen for instructions for your life, how to live holy, how to honestly accept things that only He can change, and continue from there.

- The process is to be repeated in any format you desire, but always worship Him, before closing your prayer.

- Review the model prayer in Matthew 6:9-13; Luke 11:2-4. Let Him become involved in your conviction.

Become Involved and Convicted

Prayer is one of the best activities or ministries in which one may involve themselves. It is during prayer that situations becomes durable. Begin to do short prayers that lead to longer ones. Talk with your Pastor or Leader about prayer and fasting (Matt 6:16-18). Initially, you must pray about fasting and praying. A short fast can be the first four or five hours of the morning dedicated to prayer while denying yourself food, TV time, phone time, etc. **Reminder:** please do not attempt this type of fast, if you must eat food and take medication. In this case, a modified fast is needed, i.e. abstaining from extensive phone calls, TV, sweets and other un-necessary snacks, shopping, etc. It takes faith and conviction to continue in a convicted prayer life. Faith is blind dependence on God for the outcome. Read about how the faith of a woman in Canaan changed her life in Matt. 15:1-20. Study how Jesus healed a man possessed by a demonic spirit in Mark 5:1-20. Check out how the Spirit gives wisdom in I Cor. 2:12-13.

- Get to know God! How? Through a careful private and public study of His word. Make prayer a priority for the purpose of discovering God's plans for your life through His Spiritual Gifts (I Cor. 12:4-6). Are you convicted? It is imperative for you, the prayer warrior to become wholeheartedly convinced that you should walk by faith and not by sight, through the Holy Spirit. Pray for yourself and others. Involve yourself in prayer and praying every opportunity you get. Pray for your own:

- Spiritual and physical strength,

- Your household,

- Against worldliness,

- Measures to resist sinful temptation,

- What it means to put on the whole armor of God as outlined in Ephesians 6:10-20,

- Align yourself with prayers of thanksgiving as presented in Philippians 1:2-11,
- Follow Jesus without excuse and allow the Word to come alive in you.

Become a certified Believer that Jesus is your Shepherd because you know His voice when He speaks with you. Remember, it is through ceaseless prayer that the understanding of God's planned kingdom will come. Obey and acknowledge that He created and rules the world and that your life is in His Hands. Let prayer change you for the Glory of God.

Ceaseless Prayer

Private and public prayer in ministry should be authentic and pervasive. Has prayer in ministry become routine with no evidence of Scriptural reference? If prayer is dialogue with the Triune God, how does a ministry engage in Scriptural operation without referencing the Maker and Creator? Has ministry become too modern? Is there evidence of under developed, practical skills and/or knowledge of the urgent need for ceaseless prayer? Increase your prayer practice so that your skills will increase promoting regular participation in prayer that becomes a way of life in ministry. Prayer skills are developed through daily (if not more frequent) use – using the Biblical text as a foundation. Why did the Patriots pray? Did Jesus really have to pray? After all, He is God…

Is prayer excluded from your home? In public? Is anyone praying before sharing the meal? Consider your prayer before officially retiring for the evening. Oh! You don't pray prior to retiring? Society implies that the public display of a Christian symbol (cross, fish, etc.) denotes deep spirituality and a profound prayer life. This is far from true. Again, mixed messages are conveyed when prayer is offered before the secular party begins, or before your favorite rap or Rock-N-Roll group appears to degrade every living thing and inanimate object imaginable. What happened to praying without ceasing?

Prayer Stirs People and Sets Change in Motion

By

Pastor Author James Felton, Sr. Pastor of New Revelation of Holiness Baptist Church, Chicago, IL

(Married to Drusilla Felton)

Prayer is our way to talk to God. God talks to us through his Word. We talk to Him through prayer. Pastor Herbert Lee Jr. often says "Much prayer, much power, little prayer, little power, no prayer, and no power." Seven days without prayer makes one weak. James 5:16 says, "Confess your faults one to another, and pray one for another, that ye may be healed". The effectual *fervent prayer of a righteous man availeth much". He says prayer should be effectual which means, "Producing or capable of producing an intended effect." Adequate, to sum it up is to make sure you keep the prayer line open. Psalm 66:18 says, "If I regard iniquity in my heart, the Lord will not hear me".*

Prayer should be fervent, meaning, "having or showing great warmth or intensity of spirit". There should be passion in our prayers. After all, we're talking to the God of the universe. James says, "of a righteous man" in other words, "a saved man". When you are saved, you are in a new relationship with Christ; old things have passed away, all things have become new! Sin separates us from God. When you are saved, you cannot lose you salvation, but you can lose your joy. You can break the fellowship; but where sin divides, Christ unites. He makes it possible for us to have access to God because Jesus is our intercessor. In the Old Testament, they had to make a sin offering, a peace offering, or a trespass offering, but Jesus is our sacrificial lamb. The High Priest went into the holy of holies once a year to atone for Israel's sin. But Jesus is our high priest. Hebrews 9:11 says "Neither by the blood of goats and calves, but by his own blood. He entered in once into the Holy place having obtained eternal redemption for us." Because of Jesus Christ, we can go to God in prayer. Ephesians 2:14 says, "For he is our peace, who had made both one, and hath broken down the middle wall of partition between us; verse 18 "For through him we both have access by one spirit unto the Father". In other words, because of Jesus, we can go directly to God in prayer.

Every great movement you have ever heard about throughout history, began in prayer:

- *When Isaiah told Hezekiah to get his house in order because he was going to die, Hezekiah prayed and the Lord gave him 15 more years.*

- *Assyria threatened Israel and encamped around them all night. Hezekiah prayed, went to bed, got up the next morning and found 180,000 Assyrians dead. The death angel rode and Israel never drew a bow (II Kings 19:55)*

- *Daniel was thrown into the Lion's Den, but he prayed and the Lion's den became known as "the Lion's in Daniel's Den".*

- *Paul and Silas prayed while in jail. Prayer broke the chains and unlocked the doors. The jailer and his household got saved. Acts 4:51 says that, "When they had prayed, the place was shaken where they were assembled together."*

Something happens when we pray. That's why the Devil

doesn't want you to pray. He doesn't mind you coming to church as long as you don't attend prayer meeting and Bible Study.

I don't know about you, but after this short review, I am ready to spend more time in the presence of the Lord to see what he is going to do.

(Pastor Arthur James Felton Sr., 1 Peter 5:7 "Casting all your care upon him; for he careth for you.")

In Government

Governmental changes are constant, leaving society unsure and insecure about investments, social security benefits, and other annuities. Over the past decade:

- The stock market has crashed and retirement funds have been misappropriated
- The next generations' social benefits have been compromised and threatened
- Neighborhood schools have closed at an alarming rate under the fictitious reasons of urgently needed "budget cuts".
- College tuitions have been trimmed to the bare bones
- The cost of college education has skyrocketed
- Unemployment, cut backs, layoffs, folding and failing businesses have cost home lost, family separation, community devastation and homelessness

To the prior mentioned circumstances, the nation is facing a midnight crisis. To walk through this time of darkness, prayer is the order of the day. Recall the tragedy of 9/11. It was during that time that the nation came together to pray. The then President Bush addressed the country and cited a passage from the book of Psalms. People were praying for people because prayer changes people, locations and situations. Don't forget to pray for government and government officials.

In Families

Families who once abandoned their church and faith have returned with a new dedication and commitment. They have resolved that faith in God is the only way things are going to turn around. Families are stuck without incomes and forced to exist (not live) on food from a LINK card and no cash income for rent payment. Men are walking the streets in search of "any job". The shelters are overflowing with unemployed men, broken women, innocent children and little hope. However, all is not lost. Although the City has established places of refuge, GED programs, rental assistance programs, counseling agencies and food pantries, it is insufficient based on a family's needs. The majority of the heads of households remains unemployed and many are unemployable. Thus, families are returning to their faith and the church at an alarming rate.

During altar call, not only are the parents requesting prayer, but the children and grand-children are requesting prayer for themselves. The prayer does not cease on Sunday evening, it continues until something happens or changes. The change is noted by their own follow–up testimonies of answered prayer. Prayer moves families to embrace prayer. Prayer stirs families to "HOLD ON".

In Churches

Without the stirring movement of prayer in churches, deliverance would cease, praise would become encapsulated, the gospel message would become motionless, evangelism would be halted, teaching would be meaningless and empty, the discipleship replication would be stunted and worship would fail to be authentic. Prayer is the breath of Jesus upon the ministry. Prayer sets God in motion on behalf of people, locations and situations. Because of the physical church, people are praying all over the world.

Assignment

1. "Church/state issues concern many these days. Should Christians be allowed to educate their children in church schools? Should tax money be available to such schools? What right does the government have to legislate in moral areas, such as pornography and abortion? Should Christians in communist countries be "good citizens," or revolt against oppression?

2. Not all of these questions are answered in Romans 13:1–7. But certain basic concepts about the nature and function of the state are defined here.

3. Set your group members to first, list all their church/state questions on the chalkboard, and then second, to study this passage to determine which can and which cannot be answered from it. Finally, let your group members try to establish from the passage the principles which enable them to answer some of the questions, and to give these answers".[1]

6

Prayer Will Place One In Ministry

Prayer Will Place One in Ministry

Ministry is a term applied especially to the clergy who has professed a divine call to minister in the service of any of the fivefold offices outlined by Paul (Ephesians 4:11–12):

- An apostle
- A prophet
- An evangelist
- A pastor
- A teacher

Also, similar ministry work in the church is available for all Christians (who are called by God).

"Ministry, carrying forth Christ's mission in the world, is fundamentally the task of the church, the whole → people of God, and is conferred on each Christian in → baptism. Certain persons, however, are called and ordained to ministries of leadership within the church itself. These ordained ministries, sometimes referred to as offices or holy orders, are understood differently in the various branches of the Christian church.[1]

The pattern of Christian ministry is provided by the life of Christ, who came not to receive service but to give it (Mt. 20:28; Mk. 10:45);"[2] Ministering is used in affiliation with the service within in the confines and outside the church.

The Ministry of the Word Involves the Reading and Teaching of the Word in Worship Service.

"The Minister of Christ, following the example of his Master, renders a humble but loving service to the needs of humanity at large, in the same spirit as that in which angels (Matt. 4:11; Mark 1:13) and women (Matt. 27:55; Luke 8:3) had ministered to the Lord on earth. Such service is reckoned as being done to Christ in the persons of the needy (Matt. 25:44); it is most frequently rendered to the saints (Rom. 15:25; 1 Cor. 16:15; 2 Cor. 8:4; 9:1; Heb. 6:10); but it is a mutual service within the fellowship of Christ's body (1 Pet. 4:10); and, as the ministry of the gospel (1 Pet. 1:12), it is in fact a ministry of reconciliation (2 Cor. 5:18) for the world".[3]

Start Where You Are

The believers were to be witnesses to Christ, not to themselves. They were to make disciples not to themselves but to the risen Lord (Matt. 28:18–20).[4]

Start where you are:

- Acknowledge your sins;

- Repent because you are sorry and sorrowful for your sins;

- Ask for forgiveness;

- Accept Jesus Christ as your personal Savior and God's Son;

- Believe the Gospel and pray for understanding of His word, your ministry area and to be filled with the Holy Spirit;

• The next steps: locate and attend a Bible based and Bible believing church;

• Study and attend Christian Education classes;

• Involve yourself in ministry work;

• Attach yourself to godly people;

• Abstain from ungodly practices;

• Fellowship with the saints;

• Practice what you preach;

• Discover your Spiritual gift and use it;

• Follow leadership;

• Maintain a teachable spirit;

• Accept constructive criticism, it will improve you;

• Grow in the Word;

• Become a good listener;

• Reach out to others and give, give, give;

• Finally, face your midnight, stare at it without blinking; speak to it without voice trembling; walk up to it without stumbling and embrace it as an opportunity to pray, praise and sing your way through its darkness; Midnight is simply daylight without light. Create an imagery of inner light;

Some homes are as dark as midnight, even though the lights are on, TV'S are on, candles are burning, and the play station is in full force... It is still midnight because of the condition of the hearts inside the home. The heart is the seat of our emotions, but the mind controls what enters via our thoughts.

Prayer is our way of communicating with God about our situations and circumstances. It is imperative that we pray when things are seemingly going well, or when they are going awry. Why? Because God knows the outcome in advance. Why? Because God is an omnipotent, omnipresent, and omniscient God. He is always knowledgeable about our situations and needs.

What is required to serve in the professional ministry today? Various qualifications might be mentioned. But chief among them is still the requirement of being cleansed from sin (2 Tim. 2:1, 20–21).[5]

Challenge Yourself to Find Your Secret Place

The Pastor's wife is under constant microscopic scrutiny. She is the one that is subjected to multiple complaints (fictitious or real). She is the one person in the membership that is criticized by most of the people. To her, the prior information is to be used as a tool in which holiness is demonstrated. Life is a challenge, but ministry is a charge. The charge is to live in this world, face adversities, and maintain a focus on the ministry requirements of Christ. Sounds simple? Try it.

Thus, it becomes necessary for the Pastor's wife to challenge herself to discover her secret place. The secret place in relation to challenges may be a special area of the house, the sanctuary of the church, your automobile, or during the ride to a particular destination. It could be the time spent working in the flower garden or while sitting alone in an area waiting for your husband (the pastor) to surface from his busy office. It is imperative that every opportunity is utilized to pray for God's will and desires to be manifested in her and other lives as she "models Christ" while ministering during rough times. In the meantime, other life's challenges await in the form of relationships, family and study time. The time may come when the question is asked, "Lord are you there?" Therefore, praying pastors' wives are to connect with other spiritual minded wives and activate the ministry of praying through midnight. Utilize the secret place to pray.

The women ministers are charged to pray through tumultuous times. Women ministers are often shunned by pastors seeking to only acknowledge "male ministers". This must not silence your call to preach (if you are called). It is not the woman's place to argue with others or respond to non-essential questions by other demeaning ministry members. Know that Jesus has already validated you and your call. Pray for God to prick the hearts of other believers and do not feel intimidated or threatened by the omission of extension of the opportunity to minister. Remain faithful to your call and preach the Word. Take the situation to your secret place. God will not call you to preach without providing opportunity for you to preach.

Prayerfully, examine your own experience with "self-absorption". Self-absorption speaks to the realization by others (and hopefully yourself) that ministry and ministering is "all about you." In self-absorption, the idea is to change the focus from God to you. Your focus is to have everyone "look at what you can and have done" while engaged in pseudo ministering. "I am a minister or teacher all over the city, but I am not received at my home church". "I can minister at other places, but not at my own church" "I am over-looked and under-looked because everybody is jealous of me". If the enemy is playing these types of tricks, it is time to find your secret place and pray through the darkness and self-absorption.

If you've ever assumed that God's work in the world is accomplished primarily by ordained clergy, then you need to look carefully at Jesus' words to the hometown crowd of Nazareth. "The Spirit of the Lord is upon Me," He declared, applying an Old Testament prophecy to Himself (Luke 4:18–19; Isa. 61:1–2). "Today this Scripture is fulfilled in your hearing" (Luke 4:21).

The promise fulfilled was that the Messiah had come and would do all of the things foretold in the ancient text. But the text went on to make more promises about what would happen after the Messiah's initial work: "You shall be named the priests of the Lord, they shall call you the servants of our God" (Isa. 61:6).This would be a profound change. The tasks of "ministry" would no longer be done just by priests, rabbis, or clergy, but by all of God's people. Just as the Spirit of the Lord had come upon Christ, enabling Him to accomplish God's work, so the Spirit would enable Christ's followers to accomplish God's work, too. If you are a believer in Christ, God has empowered you with His Spirit. Are you carrying out His assignments *for you?*⁶ God uses whom He wills.

We notice a startling variety of places in and out outside of Scripture where prayer took and takes place:

- In the Church or temple (Acts 3:1);
- In our prayer closet or private rooms (Acts 1:13, 14);
- Before, during, or after meetings (Acts 2:42);
- While in jail or prison (Acts 16:25);
- At the lake or on the sea or river bank (Acts 16:13);
- While fishing on the waterfront (Acts 20:36);
- On an exercise bike;
- While driving;
- While jogging or exercise in general;
- In the shower;
- By mail through letters and memos (1 Cor. 1:4);

- *"Prayer meetings: a usually informal gathering for worship and prayer especially: Protestant worship service usually held on a week night — called also prayer service*

- *On a prayer rug: a small Oriental rug used by Muslims to kneel on when praying;*

- *While using a prayer shawl: A fringed shawl traditionally worn by Jewish men at prayer. ORIGIN from Rabbinical Hebrew tallīt, from biblical Hebrew tillel 'to cover'⁷;*

- *"Ritual Garments include the requirement of a head covering for all males and for married females, especially during prayer and study. Most often, men wear a kipah or yarmulke (skullcap). During morning prayers, men tra-*

*ditionally wear a tallit (prayer shawl with ritually knot-
ted fringes at the four corners) and, on weekdays only,
tefillin (phylacteries, small leather boxes on the forehead
and upper arm containing slips of parchment on which
are written the relevant biblical commandments, like the
passage containing Deut. 6:8)."*[8]

*"The fringes on the borders of the robes were meant to
hang from the corners of the upper garment (Deut. 22:12),
which was worn on top of the clothing. The tassel was
probably made by twisting the overhanging threads of the
garment into a knot that would hang down. The tassels
were retained down through history, and today more elaborate prayer shawls with tassels are worn during prayer.
The blue color may represent the heavenly origin of the
Law, or perhaps, since it is a royal color, the majesty of
the Lord*[9].

*"The tassel is a dangling ornament of white wool-
en threads and a blue cord attached to the four corners
of one's garment as a reminder of God's presence, salvation, and commandments in accordance with the instructions given in Num. 15:38–41 (Heb. ṣîṣit; KJV "fringe");
Deut. 22:12 (gᵉdilîm; KJV "fringes"). With the decline in
the wearing of four-cornered garments, the tallit or prayer
shawl, with tassels attached to the corners in a prescribed
elaborate fashion, came to be worn by Jewish men during
daytime prayer times. Many modern Orthodox Jewish men
also wear the tallit katan, a smaller tallit with tassels, under
their shirts. It may have been the tassels of Jesus' garment
that the woman with a hemorrhage touched (Matt. 9:20
par.) and that were the means of healing for others (14:36
par.); Gk. kráspedon (RSV "fringe[s]") might represent
simply the edge of Jesus' garment (KJV "border, hem") or
the distinctive Jewish tassels, referred to in 23:5"*[10]

*"The New Testament has some sharp statements
about the Pharisees' and scribes' punctiliousness over
ritual regulations, while ignoring the heart of the Torah
(see Matt. 23). The people of the land would have hearti-
ly agreed with such utterances. An example of that is the
occasion when Jesus' disciples were eating without having
washed their hands (Mark 7:1–13 par Matt. 15:1–9). It*

was not that the people of the land were opposed to clean-liness; they simply did not follow the rules strictly". [11]

The blue color may represent the heavenly origin of the Law, or perhaps, since it is a royal color, the majesty of the LORD. *This was a reminder of the covenant.*

• *Pray with a prayer partner over the phone prayer line.*

"For most people, however, a special place for private prayer is helpful. Henri Nouwen tells about the importance to him of the poustinia. Poustinia is a Russian word that means hermitage. Nouwen has applied the concept of hermitage to his everyday living. While teaching at Yale, he lived in an apartment with a huge walk-in closet. Being a priest, he had a limited wardrobe and no need for that much space. He converted it to a prayer closet." [12]

"The simple fact that I'm in the closet means I'm praying," he says. "I might have a thousand things to think about while I'm in there, but the fact that I'm sitting in this physical place means I'm praying. I force myself to stay there for fifteen minutes. I do my best to center my mind and clear it of distracting thoughts and get down to prayer, but if after fifteen minutes I haven't been entirely success-ful, I say, 'Lord this was my prayer, even all this confusion. Now I'm going back to the world'. "The New Testament does not condemn the wearing of a phylactery or fringes on a prayer-shawl as such (Matt. 23:5). What it does condemn is the Jewish authorities' rejection of Jesus, and the way they imposed what, from a Christian point of view, were paltry regulations on the people. The scribes accused the people of the land of neglecting the instruction of the Torah, but they themselves interpreted it unilaterally". [13]

Change Your Location

Consider changing your spiritual and physical location. A spiritual location change has to do with renewing your mind in light of the Word. Satan will enter the mind, first, but Paul teaches that we should let Christ's mind be in us. Many pompous and prideful acts and thoughts begin with a simple thought. Because the thought is self-centered and feeds our own ego, it advances and becomes larger and larger. The results…you are out of control and out of the will of God. This is a good time to change the mental as well as the physical location so that the focus is on God and His Word. Try focusing on the Word, the Work and the Worship.

A physical location change may become necessary to inspire behavioral change. Your surroundings may have an effect on your behavior. Change may become physical in an effort to re-establish and re-build your physical self. Physical well-being combined with mental stability are prescriptions for healing the emotional and physical instability. For example, when one is delivered from substance abuse, it is wise not to hang with the friends that are continuing to use after you have broken free via deliverance. It is time for a location change.

A Place of Ministry and Ministering

The church is where growth and transformation should take place in believers. The church is a place of nourishment that promotes our growth toward Christ's likeness by one another. As believers, we are to encourage others honestly, address adverse behaviors, teach with integrity, and demonstrate love to all in all situations. The church is where we learn and teach disciples how to minister while ministering. Ministry leaders are developed in small groups. For example, the Usher Board Ministry is an excellent opportunity to develop into ministry. How? Because it requires people skills, the exercise of tact and restraint, the need to follow directions and the need to demonstrate universal kindness to all entering the sanctuary. That love and growth includes strangers with an alteration in their attitude in the same manner that God accepts and loves us with our strange attitudes (that is not from Him). We are to discern and practice God's own acceptance and love, and grow. Paul explains that we are to *"Grow up into ... Christ".* *Paul called it in Ephesians 4:15, growing up, together, into Christ.*

Assignment

Ask your group members to rank on a scale of 1 to 10 the importance of the following:

1. People accept me as I am _____.
2. I feel loved and wanted_____.
3. I can share with those close to me_____.
4. When I make mistakes, others don't condemn or reject me___.
5. I don't have to be just like everyone else to be welcome____.
6. I am valued and make a real contribution to others_____.
7. I don't have to compete but can cooperate with others_____.

Discuss the rankings, encouraging your group members to share why the high importance items are significant to them. Then move into the text, explaining that each item describes what the church of Christ is to be like—and these passages show us how to build just this kind of vital Christian fellowship.[14]

If you had to write steps to Christian Growth, what would you write? Go ahead, list your steps...

7

Sincere Prayer Changes Midnight Situations

Lost in the Church

If Jesus is the church and we are in Him, are we not part of the church?
If Jesus is the church and we are in Him and we are a part of the church, do we not mimic His character?
If Jesus is the church and we are in Him and we are a part of the church, do we not only mimic His character, but have we been changed?
If Jesus is the church and we are in Him and we are a part of the church, do we not mimic His character because we are changed, but because we are not lost in the church?
We often lose things in our own house, but when we do, we search for it until it is found. When we have believers who are lost in the house, we must send out an arrest warrant for their capture and conviction. Believers believe that Jesus was born, He ministered, He died and He rose again, but if they are lost in the church, they have no convictions. Those believers should be captured and arrested as perpetrators. Those believers are pretenders who are inside the house, but still lost—in the house (church).
Believers are lost in the church because their praise is lost at the 11:00 a.m. hour and found at the party by 11:00 p.m. the same day. They need to check their salvation. When believers sing, "He can work it out" on Sunday evening and try to work it out themselves on Monday, a spiritual check is necessary. If believers don't trust God, the maker and Creator of the house, they could be lost in His house. Qualify your house…
(By R. Messenger, 2005)

Sincere Prayer Changes Midnight Situations

Changes make one take notice of different situations, particular circumstances, new positions, transformations or new directions. When one is pressed for certain information, it may conclude with a change of subject. It is a common saying in the church that "when it is time for the offering, most worshippers will request change for a five so that they can give the usual one dollar contribution". Like changing a small bill to contribute an even smaller bill, when one's mood changes, it is noted by others as a person passing from one phase to another, expecting change for the small things.

The same with midnight situations that are not committed to prayer. It causes a change in one's tomorrows. It alters situations and it modifies the attitude for the worst. Prayer makes a difference, don't ask for change, but press toward growth.

"CHANGE implies making either an essential difference often amounting to a loss of original identity or a substitution of one thing for another. ALTER implies a difference in some particular respect without suggesting loss of identity. VARY stresses a breaking away from sameness, duplication, or exact repetition. MODIFY suggests a difference that limits, restricts, or adapts to a new purpose." [12]

Therefore, spiritual change makes a difference, alters the condition of our minds, stresses duplication of Christ's character and ultimately causes a sincere change that modifies our midnight situations.

The Midnight Situations

Midnight is when dormant childhood abuse is awakened and promotes feelings of abandonment by seemingly uncaring parents, relatives and friends. Immediately, the feeling of personal failure is at the forefront of life. That familiar empty feeling surfaces. The mistrust and feeling of being cheated and mistreated becomes the new preoccupation. Depression creeps in. The inner plotting begins to set your life of buried memories on a downward spiral. The questions begin: "What did I do? What can I do? Who do I tell? Will they believe me? Is this real or not? Who will I hurt, if I tell who hurt me? Am I involved in a bad dream? Do my parents really care? Why was I born to such uncaring parents? What about my siblings? Perhaps I was adopted? Lord, do you hear me? My nights are restless. My days are filled with uncertainty. Time is passing slowly. The nights are long and time is standing still. Lord, are you still there? I cannot hear you!"

For every action, there is a reaction. Otherwise, something else will follow. What you do will impact your circumstances. When looking at the whole picture, it is crowded. Therefore, it is essential that one item at a time is viewed. Dissect the problem and address it in small chunks. It is time to locate and trust a person. The new trend is to call a hotline to vent and obtain counseling information. That may be an option. Also, there are 24-hour prayer lines to pray you through the night. Relief is on the way. For example, when you began to be-haviorally and verbally become thankful, more will come, and your circumstances will either change, or you will view them differently. Conviction will show you what could have taken place, but didn't. God will show you that He is in control and has already predestined your life. Do not wait, start now because God is soon to return: Moses saw it; Joshua believed it; Jeremiah prophesied it; Paul preached it; Luke taught it; Mark declared it; Revelation speaks of it; He is return-ing soon. Until His return, pray from your secret place and involve a trusted person in the situation.

Which of the following characterizes your situation?

- You feel deep guilt for willful sin that perhaps has even ruined your own or someone else's life (as you see it). See David's prayer after he committed the sins of adul-tery and murder (Ps. 51).

- When feeling frightened by responsibilities that seem totally beyond your skills and ability. Review Moses' "dialogue" with God (Ex. 3:1–4:17).

- If you are bound by the feeling of frustration and anger over injustice from a local, national, and international level and is wondering why God doesn't seem to intervene, read the Book of Habakkuk.

- When there is fear of a family member's hostility over wrongs that you have done, read Jacob's story of how he called out to God for safety from his brother Esau (Gen. 32:9–12; 33).

- Position problems: You have been threatened by someone who thinks you are out to take over their power and position. David has a solution (Ps. 57, 142).

- Unfairness and prejudices in combination with persecution because you are a Christian. There is a prayer for boldness that the early church prayed after its leaders had been jailed and threatened (Acts 4:13–31).

- A child is stricken with an incurable illness and you are forced to stand idly by and powerless to help. The Syro-Phoenician woman offers insight to your problem – she pled her case with Jesus for mercy (Matt. 15:21–28).

- You are troubled by a chronic physical sickness and have not obtained healing. What did Paul do? He appealed his case to God for healing (2 Cor. 12:7–10)

- There is no one solution or method for expressing yourself to God, but he hears arguments, pleas, and pain. He also takes pleasure in hearing our joys, praises, and elations. Give yourself to the God who listens and wait for his reply.

The Holy Spirit's Inspiration

The Holy Spirit is a person with a personality, not an "it" and He is the inspiration for prayer. It is the intelligence of the Holy Spirit that stirs life in a forward movement that pleases God. There is never an instance that sites that the Holy Spirit misled or misguided anyone at any time. He (the Holy Spirit) dissolves midnight situations and leads us through our valley experiences. The Spirit is what Jesus left to teach and guide believers in all areas of life. The Holy Spirit leads believers through valley experiences, healing from terminal diseases, returns wayward children, prevents accidents, provides protection, warnings, etc. The Holy Spirits inspires and helps us to pray and live holy lives.

Examples From Real Life Situation

The Holy Spirit speaks to real life situations, such as this writer's. Read my (R. Messenger's) personal journey from a 1998 journal. It shows evidence that the Holy Spirit remains active.

What has prayer changed for you lately? All of my life, I have been told that prayer changes things. In my childhood years, I wondered, "what has prayer changed for me lately? What?" It does not seem to work, but my mother declared that it did:

- I was born into poverty. Every day was a new struggle and adventure

- A balanced diet was out of the question and "hand-me-downs" were the new Saks Fifth Avenue, in our home

- I lived in a shack (a shot gun house), but we knew Jesus and attended church weekly

- The family lived in one or two rooms with a kitchen and maybe a living room. The playroom was the back yard (with no grass) or an open field. The outside washroom was the bomb of the south. The kitchen doubled as a dining area and formal dining room. We were happy and obedient to our mom.

- I had no rich or even well-to-do relatives of which to ask for the finer things of life

- I did not even have a father in the home

- I had no fancy clothes. As a matter of fact, I wore patched jeans and shoes with wired soles. No shoe shop for us. But, my mom said, "Prayer changes things. We will be okay". As I got older, I prayed to the best of my knowledge and ability. Prayer seemed to make things worse (so I thought) but I continued to pray because my mom said, "Prayer works, baby".

- As children, we were required to work long hard hours in the fields. Ends still did not meet, but we were happy.

- We chopped cotton in the heat, picked cotton in the cold, planted watermelon with a wood handled hoe, picked squash in the rain and pulled corn in the dead of the frost season. Mom was beside us, talking, teaching, singing her hymns and praying.

- We were paid $2.50 to $3.00 per day (not an hour) and that went for food and other bare necessities, but we pooled our resources and shared.

- My mother finally got a better job. She began working for the "white folk," cooking, washing, ironing, bowing, scraping and saying, "Yes ma'am" and "no sir" to their babies. What had prayer changed for me? I went with her to work one day (because I was the oldest girl at home) and her job did not work for me. I swept the floor, mopped the floor, then I was tired. So I took a nap, underneath the bed. Mom discovered that I was not working and decided that I should continue my education. I did. That ended my housekeeping career.

- Well, as time slowly passed, we still had nothing. School was interesting, when I had the opportunity to attend. We were required to stay out during the crop season to help with the farming. My mom did not understand that I had to "take my tests and submit my home work as instructed to pass to the next grade." Yet, she stressed education. She spent hours teaching me phonics while she did the ironing using an iron that was heated on the fire. I would read to her and she would teach me how to pronounce difficult words. By the way, mom had a fourth grade education.

- Everybody in town had a T.V., and at least one old beat up car, but us.

- The other girls could go out with their friends or for a ride in their "boyfriend's" car, but not us. The girls could not go because, "nice" girls did not do that. Most of the other girls ended up in trouble, but not us. We were home listening to mom pray.

- Other children attended dances and after school functions, but we did not. If my mom had permitted me to go, I would not have had anything to wear anyway... So you know what we were doing? Yes, we were listening to mom pray.

- I borrowed my first prom dress and had to be in the house by midnight. Incidentally, my mom interviewed my date and obtained his family history before permitting me to go to prom in his grandfather's old beat up car. I think his grandfather was about 80 years old at the time and his car reflected his age. Imagine how old the car was. Of course, "I was embarrassed by my mom's investigation". She meant business and I was home by 11:45 p.m., but not the other girls... they stayed and got into trouble, but you know where I was. That's correct! Home listening to my mom pray, lecture and sing.

- Other children seemed to have gotten away with murder, but if we stumped one toe, the neighbor tried to break it, I would limp home with one toe hurting to discover that the neighbor had told my mom and she tried to break the other nine. Mom was 4' 11" and did not play at all. Ask my brothers. For many years, I believe they had chills when they saw a broom.

- I played basketball, partly because I was relatively good at it and partly because I could get out of the sight of my mom's discipline and lectures for a few hours.

- I rode the bus to some basketball games, but it seemed that the teachers only watched me and who I sat next to during the ride. They would actually tell my mom!

- As we became older, my next older brother began to date. That left me stuck with doing his high school homework assignments (I was in the eighth grade). I actually began to enjoy it.

- I hated wash days at my house. Mom would line up 2-3 metal tubs on the front porch. We had to carry the water, heat the water, boiled the white clothes, wash the quilts, cook the starch, hang the clothes out on the line to dry, wash the curtains, and clean everything that was not nailed down, by the time the laundry was completed. Incidentally, my brothers never cooked (not even to warm up the food), did not do laundry, dishes, wash, iron, make beds, swept or mopped the floors. They were responsible for the outside work because "men did not do ladies work".

- Note: I needed prayer to hurry up and change things in all our lives

- We rarely attended Sunday school or Bible class (no transportation). The preacher lived in another city and we lived in the country. He did not show up for class and neither did we...? But we went to church with our mom. She never sent us by anyone else, she took us herself.

- My father was rarely around, because he worked on the railroad and had very little time home. But he always said that I was "different."

So what did prayer do for the family? Prayer shaped and molded our family. Today, we continue to attend church and pray, all of us. Thank God for my mom.

We remember mom as a strong and steadfast praying mom who carried a gun in her apron pocket and kept one behind the headboard of her bed, because no one was going to mess with her girls. With all that said and done, I made it on the wings of my mother's prayers. Since that time, I have discovered that my mother's prayers were stored up for me and I am continuing to reap the benefits of a praying mother, because sincere prayer did change our Midnight situations. Today, I am thankful that I am enjoying the daylight. I am thankful that I was able to accept Jesus and His plan for my life. The morning feels so good...

Examples From the Biblical Text

The Biblical text provides examples of how Midnight issues and real life changes happened... because the change was Holy Spirit inspired:

- *2 Sam. 7:27 For you, O Lord of hosts, the God of Israel, have made this revelation* to your servant, saying, 'I will build you a house.' Therefore your servant has found courage to pray this prayer to you.*

- *1 Kings 8:28 Yet have regard to the prayer of your servant and to his plea, O Lord my God, listening to the cry and to the prayer that your servant prays before you this day,*

- *1 Kings 8:29 that your eyes may be open night and day toward this house, the place of which you have said, 'My name shall be there,' that you may listen to the prayer that your servant offers toward this place.*

- *1 Kings 8:38 whatever prayer, whatever plea is made by any man or by all your people Israel, each knowing the affliction of his own heart and stretching out his hands toward this house.*

- *1 Kings 8:54 Now as Solomon finished offering all this prayer and plea to the Lord, he arose from before the altar of the Lord, where he had knelt with hands outstretched toward heaven.*

- *Luke 1:13 But the angel said to him, "Do not be afraid, Zechariah, for your prayer has been heard, and your wife Elizabeth will bear you a son, and you shall call his name John.*

- *Rom. 10:1 Brothers, my heart's desire and prayer to God for them is that they may be saved.*

- *Jas. 5:16 Therefore, confess your sins to one another and pray for one another, that you may be healed. The prayer of a righteous person has great power as it is working. (KJV)*

The Situation Changed Through Prayer

By

Mildred J. Bonds, Intercessor

Holy Rock Church & Outreach Ministries, Chicago, IL 60621

"My Midnight"

    Prayer has become an integral part of my life. I cannot imagine my life without prayer. However, there was a time I would not have been able to make such a statement with the faith and confidence I now have. This was not always the case. There have been many midnights in my life, but there is one in particular that stands above the rest. This is the one that forced me to become serious about praying. Why midnight? Because, it was figuratively so dark that I couldn't see or feel my way out. I felt so isolated and alone. It was as though I was in a room full of people, but yet invisible. I couldn't hear anyone and no one could hear me. The deafness that engulfed the room prevented my voice from being heard and therefore no one was able to respond to my crisis. It was at this time, I realized I needed someone far greater and wiser than man. I needed God. In the midst of my midnight, just for a moment, a thought came to me, pray child, pray.

    This midnight experience was the first and last of this kind and it left a lasting imprint in the recess of my mind and transformed my life forever. The reason it had such an impact on my life was because it was "scary" and not of a natural origin. If it had been, I could have consulted a doctor and adhered to his recommendation and be done. Sounds simple enough, but not so, because again it was of the spiritual realm and therefore, of a spiritual nature. I had been thrown into a spiritual battle with zero knowledge or understanding of what was forthcoming. You see, before this happened, I was basically satisfied with my life and how things were going. But within a matter of minutes, my life was turned upside down. I can't tell you what words I prayed, but I can tell you I sought God in every way I knew how. As I continue, let me explain what led to these chains of events. I had just made up my mind to become more serious about my relationship with God. To prove to myself I was ready and prepared to make such a commitment, I attended a prayer meeting at the church. Attending church on a week night was unheard of during this phase of my life.

What happen next sent my life spiraling out of control. It was during the prayer meeting that I was attacked by the enemy, at least through my eyes; this was the work of the enemy, Satan, himself. I say this because I was attacked by a spirit of depression, a spirit of heaviness, and a spirit of fear. I was unable to comprehend what was happening to me. I became so depressed. It was a daily struggle to get out bed and every task, no matter how small became a monumental challenge. I begin to suffer from sleep deprivation and hallucination. I couldn't concentrate and as a result often time left work early. I felt like someone or something had literally taken the mental and emotional burden of others and placed them on me. It got so bad until I felt life was no longer life as I knew life to be. I just wanted to die and get it over with. I had concluded this would be the only way I could get some relief, some peace. But, because God is God, and this would prove to be a part of His ultimate plan, He provided me with a way of escape. My will to live and regain my sanity became greater than my will to die.

I begin to see the darkness leave and the light enter. God had rescued me. I started to read the bible daily. I found myself in church every time the doors opened. I prayed morning, noon and night. I can't tell you what words I prayed, just that I prayed. I watched every religious program on television that even remotely addressed the topics of healing and deliverance. I read book after book on those same topics. I wanted to be free. It's nothing like being in an invisible prison with no keys to get out. Over time and through determination, perseverance, faith and patience, I discovered the keys that would open the door to freedom. Once the door was open, what seemed like a lifetime was over. My darkness turned to light. My sadness turned to joy. My torments turned to peace. My craziness turned to sanity. My apathy turned to empathy. My midnight was over. I was looking for relief, but

I received so much more. Now when I say pray, I say it with conviction and I pray with fervor. I pray with a sincere and contrite heart.

The midnights will come and go, but it won't last, because joy will come in the morning. I'm a living witness! I have a reminder from God that He was always there. He gave me the scripture, Psalm 34:1, I will bless the Lord at all times and His praise shall continually be in my mouth. God bless, M. J. Bonds, Intercessor.

Assignment

Expound on each bullet point. When I develop a divine viewpoint:

• I will be released from jealousy.

• I will discover fulfillment in being who "I am", rather than wanting to be like "someone" else.

• My friendships will not distort my status—I am awed by none, and look down on none.

• I will appreciate others for themselves, without feeling they must be different or must be like me.

I will learn to take God's view of others as members with me in a body where cooperation, not competition, has value. I will initiate a whole new way of relating to others and become unlike any person the world has ever known.

"This is the first key to building a righteous, loving community. To see ourselves and others as God does, as valuable contributing persons in a family of faith".[3]

8

When Men Pray, A Change Will Come

When Men Pray, a Change Will Come

Books have been written, testimonies are accessible, CD's and DVD's are readily available, wives are celebrating the change, and children are following pursuit... because men are praying and consequently, changes have come into their lives. When men pray, change is inevitable. David had his mighty men. They were set aside and distinguished in their loyalty to David. The pastor is a David type that has the charge to lead men to Jesus, the King. Jesus is assembling His mighty men, women, and children to build His earthly kingdom.

However, it is mandatory that we adhere to the "quality improvement standards" along with other requirements.

The requirements are as follows:

(1) Honor is the recognition of a good reputation. The "good reputation" must proceed the person. It is similar to a component of a resume. It is what an employer is requesting from a perspective employee. To verify the person's position of "honor", references are requested to validate what is written. The pastor must be able to verify the person's position of honor through prayerful observation and meticulous evaluation of their ministry work record. A tarnished reputation results in a position of dishonor rather than honor. Today, many famous political and societal figures have tarnished reputations and work ethics because of their failure to resist temptation and abuse of power. Many are fascinated with position and status. Without holy restraints, men may be overtaken in lust for more power, producing unhealthy results: substance abuse, immersing themselves in the fast lane of life and ultimately failing to "put God first". The end results is a "power failure" that the utility company is unable to restore.

(2) Duty is respect and moral judgment of the professing saint. Respect begins with one's self and moves outward to become

an example to others and a way of life.

(3) Love is unconditional and not manipulative.

(4) Strong faith is the eye that sees the invisible and the hand that reaches for God's promises. Strong faith ushers in strong confidence in God.

(5) Love is unselfish. A selfish person cannot be a hero.

(6) Consistent, earnest and intense prayerfulness shows "power connection" with God and with men" (Gen. 32:28).

(7) Wisdom is from God to man.

(8) A courageous person has the ability to lead without fear of man, but of God.

(9) Leadership is the ability to fellowship, go ahead, plan ahead, by knowing that God is the Head.

(10) Work is a living faith in action. "Faith without works is dead faith".

We should not be content just to exist as Christians, but should aim to be "mighty." This is possible to all, through union with the "strong Son of God," maintained and increased by vigorous exercises of faith, meditation, and prayer; and through faithful use of such power as they possess. Whatever our might or achievements, we should ascribe all, and be sincerely concerned that others should ascribe all, to God. (Verse 10, 12.)—G. W.[1]

The Results of Pastor's Empowering Men to Pray

Empowering is the process of transferring legal authority or other forms of power from one person to another (in this instance). It is increasing godly self-actualization, self-worth, and self-esteem to men under the tutelage of a God fearing Pastor. Pastors are charged with an incredible responsibility. They are the watchmen for our souls. They are the spiritual nurturer while we are yet, in the incubator. The pastor lives out the process of understanding and knowing the Word that will nourish us. For this on-going task, prayer is a requirement, not an option. It is the process of accepting men where they are and moving them to where they should be. It involves long conversations, godly examples, mentoring, leadership that culminates into empowerment. Empowering is planning and evaluation: Assignments and tasks; leadership and headship; study, faith and works; and trust, obedience and victory. Finally, it takes time, energy, more prayer, fellowship and discipleship replication to move men from stagnation to maturity. The pastor is charged with the duties and responsibilities of implementing the challenge, but men are called to accept and follow the challenger. Prayer will change the hearts of men because

Elders/overseers are responsible for instruction in and defense of the faith (1 Tim. 3:9; 4:11–13; 5:17; 2 Tim. 2:2; 3:16–17; Titus 1:9; 2:1, 15), the administration of worship and related activities (1 Tim. 2:1–8; 5:3–16), oversight of the discipline and restoration of sinning members (1 Tim. 5:20, 22), and the successful transfer of the ministry to a new generation of faithful men (2 Tim. 2:2). Some may have a more concentrated role of communicating the Word of God than others (1 Tim. 5:17)[2]

So, the pastor must lead with integrity. The word integrity is a 14th century word that means honesty, incorruptibility by the adherence to a standard of moral and undivided Biblical values.

"The pastor must live and minister with integrity amid all of the pressures of society. The heavy weight of maintaining a high standard is consistent with the recognition that God requires more of us because he has given much to us". African American Church Management Handbook (p.33)[3]

In addition, the pastor must become a manager. He must manage his own household well. *An elder "Leadership within the home, especially in relationship to his children, help indicate whether a leader is able to lead God's children in His household.[4]*

The Pastor/leader must not be quick tempered, but patient. He must be slow to anger, unselfish, not insecure with feelings of inferiority. It is of the utmost importance that he has clear judgment and free from "drunkenness"; must not have and addictive behavior (that may lure him away from his calling or duties); not a violent man, but exercises self-control; balanced and pursues honesty; not for dishonest gain, but maintains an above reproach attitude regarding money, and hospitality (love expressed). The pastor/leader must communicate the gospel message and lead an upright and un-polluted life as evidenced by the exercise of gentleness when dealing with people and,

"Excellence of reputation with the unbelieving community protects one from falling "into disgrace and into the devil's trap." The world needs no ammunition, which can be aimed toward the church

as an excuse for their unbelieving responses. Protecting the reputation of the gospel continues to be a priority emphasis in the Pastoral Epistles".[5]

For pastors and leaders alike, integrity is not an option, it is a mandate to remain free from compromise. Remember, because Satan is who he is, there will always be opportunities to venture outside the central model set forth in the Scriptures. David did it! Jacob's mother fell for it. Solomon forgot it. Samson failed it. Saul permitted a jealous spirit to weaken it. Apostles pray for it. Bishops seek it. But pastors must not blow it. Prayers, in combination with the Word are the two practices that will keep men focused. Reminder:

"Two men, two acts, two results. Just as Adam's disobedience brought sin and death to the world (5:12, 18), Christ's obedience brought righteousness and life (5:18–21). In a long parenthetical statement (5:13–17), Paul highlighted the contrast between Adam and Christ:

Because of the sin of one man, Adam, every human has experienced both physical and spiritual death (see Gen. 3:19; Eph. 2:1). Because of the righteousness of one man, Jesus Christ, every human can experience eternal life (see 1 Cor. 15:22). Paul explained once again how the law brings not righteousness but awareness of sin (5:20; compare 3:20); the more we are aware of sin, the more we can cast ourselves on God's grace."[6]

Man's Responsibility From the Text and in Real Life Situations

According to the book of Ephesians, husbands should love their wives, (both husbands and wives must submit and love). To live holy.

"Husbands, love your wives, as Christ loved the church and [7h]gave himself up for her", Ephesians 5: 25.[8] Though the husband's authority has been established (vv. 22–24), the emphasis moves to the supreme responsibility of husbands in regard to their wives, which is to love them with the same unreserved, selfless, and sacrificial love that Christ has for His church. Christ gave everything He had, including His own life, for the sake of His church, and that is the standard of sacrifice for a husband's love of his wife. [9]

Men are to be self-disciplined.

The order of creation and deception at the Fall argue for male responsibility in different ways. The order of creation is plain enough. At the Fall, both the deception of Eve and the fact that responsibility still rested with Adam argue again for male leadership. Though Eve sinned first and was deceived, sin was passed on to the human race through Adam (Rom. 5:12). [10] (Therefore, just as sin came into the world through one man, and death through sin, and so death spread to all men because all sinned)[11]

Men are:

- To imitate Christ's character and lead the family in prayer

- To be a father and role model to his children

- To love his wife

- To humble himself

- To be courageous

- To exercise patience

- To promote good works

- To remain sincere in sound doctrine and speech

- To be humble and determined to stand as a man

- To practice proper sexual control

- To serve as a godly example of a man

- To serve and revere God as the Creator

- To be sober and right minded

- To be honest and temperate

- To be self-controlled and sound in faith

The Biblical text is filled with examples of godly men who exhibited short times of failure, fear and weakness, but God did not write them off. However, the focus of this section is on examples of godly men from the text. God created male and female in His image and likeness. Thus, the text presents man in both failures and weaknesses, successes and failures, and tells of their incompleteness without women to share in their lives. Yet, men have been given specific tasks and responsibilities by God.

Examples of Godly men from the Text

- Noah in Genesis 6:9

- Abraham in Genesis 22:1-12

- Moses in Exodus 32:30-32

- David in 1 Samuel 24:1-7

- Hezekiah in 2 King 18:1-7

- Job in Job 1:1-8

- Daniel in Daniel 6:10

- Stephen in Acts 7:54-60

The Church Holding Men Responsible

It must be clearly understood that Christ is the head of the Church. He has determined set leaders in the church to facilitate the growth and maturity of the church through Christ. The church must be obedient to Christ. The church (Christ) holds men responsible for its movement. The Holy Spirit is the director of the Church. Leaders are appointed, but God calls and equips them. The church (Christ) holds man responsible as follows: To adhere to His call to leadership, evangelism, pastor, teacher, elders (as leaders) and deacons. The man as church leader is to preach the Word, teach the unadulterated Gospel, provide directions in the church, train and appoint other leaders, ensure discipline is exercised in the church, support leaders financially, submit to leadership, build up the church, discern true and false teaching, and pray for the sick. "Those who have served well gain an excellent standing and great assurance in their faith in Christ Jesus" (v. 13).[12]

Man, Return to Your Place

God can work wonders if He can get a suitable man. Men can work wonders if they allow God to lead them. The full endowment of the Spirit that turned the world upside down would be eminently useful in these latter days. Men who can stir things mightily for God, whose spiritual revolutions change the whole aspect of things, are the universal need of the Church.[13]

A man's assignment is to live in God's Word and abstain from ungodly unions and immoral behaviors (i.e. Genesis 19:4). Man is not to:

- Participate in ungodly behaviors against God's leaders,

- Should be equally yoked in marriage,

- Should not be a spiritual or physical killer,

- Should keep magic, hexes, fortune telling, voodoo, etc. out of his life,

- Should not be a rebel against Biblical life-style teachings and doctrine,

- Should become devoted to prayer and to the ministry of the word,

- Should understand and practice the ministry of righteousness,

- Should submit to headship and leadership.

Moving Men, Ministries and Mending Communities

Men are to struggle for excellence through Christ. All un-crucified areas of imperfection will fester and escalate to cause human error or a major crash that will negatively impact other's lives. Deficient men (humanity) fail to:

- Attend to details by not paying attention

- Throw precaution to the wind because of failure to pay attention

- Listen, but hear or adhere

- Read the instructions because real men use their head, not directions

- Rules are made for others to follow, not a real man. Real men make the rules, not follow them…

- Rebels and listens to the beat of a different drummer…

- Becomes resentful when others excel and they don't, especially

What a recipe for a human race wreck! However, the human race seems not to have learned from prior deadly wreck in the garden. How do you survive a "head on collision with God?" Answer… it takes His Grace and Mercy for your survival. Examples of on-going collisions and wrecks are: requesting to be like others, failure to pay tithes and give a liberal offerings, grumbling against leadership, fornication, adultery, jealousy, poor judgment, lust for richness, failure to pray and keep God's law, failure to teach the children and bring them up in the fear of the Lord, lying, cheating, stealing, abuse of authority, and the list goes on. Are YOU on a collision course and headed for a head on collision or wreck? Check your direction and return to the teachings of Jesus. Of course, humans are not perfect, but it is a desire and a goal to press toward the mark and live holy. We are to work toward spiritual maturity through Jesus. Immaturity causes life wrecks.

Moving Men, Ministries and Mending Communities

By

Apostle H. L. Messenger, Sr. Pastor and CEO of Holy Rock Church & Outreach Ministries

Moving men, ministries and mending communities are on this wise; one cannot expect a car to move, if it is not in gear. So, it is with men. Men cannot expect to move forward without a purpose, motivation and an objective.

Men have been in low gear (or no gear) too long. Our European brothers would have us to think that we only have one gear and that gear is reverse. If men move forward, ministry will take place and communities will be mended. How are men going to accomplish this major task? First, men must understand the concept that will move men. Second, the concept must cause the development of a right attitude. Third, the concept and the right attitude must be mixed with a determination to change. Fourth, a team is needed. Fifth, a team effort must be implemented.

A team effort involves understanding the concept of division. Division brings on burdens. Burdens are heavy. However, together, a team of men are able to come together and make the burdens lighter. For example, if one is carrying a hundred pound load, it may be too heavy for one man, but if fifty men are assisting that man with the one-hundred pound load, each man is only responsible for carrying two pounds, which makes the load considerably lighter. Thus, the journey becomes easier and the team effort becomes a cohesive mending process.

As communities are mended through ministries, men must not forget past struggles and pain. Men have been burdened down, pushed back and someone said, "Hit harder than a baseball", but with God's help, men are able to push and praise beyond the pain. Remember, men are to stand as Holy men in unity, a team!

The men of Holy Rock Church & Outreach Ministries are joined together as a team engaged in an "on-going forward" ministry. We are called the "20 Plus Men." These "20 Plus Men" will form the "1000 plus men". We are not limited to a specific number of men! What we aim to do is exit the circle and "reach out" (to the outside). We are to continue reaching by training other men to reach out. No one should be left out because every man is reaching for someone else. Thus, the goal of this mentoring ministry is to "Mentor young men" by:

1. *Bringing them into a right relationship with God*

2. *Empowering them to change through prayer and the Word*

3. *Encouragement for their efforts*

4. *Motivating them through men of integrity*

5. *Teaching new skills for the journey*

6. *Ministering in and to the community*

7. *Mending broken relationships*

Finally, the children and the forth coming generations will come to the knowledge and ability to continue to do great works. This will continue to bring hope and restoration to not just the Englewood and surrounding communities, but to other communities, citywide because "Iron Sharpens Iron." Blessings to the team–Apostle H. L. Messenger

Assignment

In this area, Paul gives several practical suggestions: Explain the meaning of each assignment.

"Whatever you believe about these things keep between yourself and God".

"Make every effort to do what leads to peace and mutual edification".

"We who are strong ought to bear with the failings of the weak and not to please ourselves" The goal toward which we are to work, giving it priority rather than convictions, is "that with one heart and mouth you may [together] glorify the God and Father of our Lord, Jesus Christ".

Youth / Adult

To help your group members explore this significant passage on Christian living, duplicate and give to teams of five or six member's one of these two case histories. Each team is to study Romans 14:1–15:7, identify principles which might apply to its case, and then tell how they might be applied to help the people involved in the case history.

Case 1: Linda's children are in school now, and she wants to go back to work. Her husband, Jim, opposes. He feels that it's a man's place to earn the family living, and that Linda should find fulfillment in her role as a wife and mother. Each feels very strongly about this situation, and each goes to the Bible to suggest he or she is right.

Case 2: Bob spoke in his class to express his doubts about drinking. Wine was drunk in Bible times. Drunkenness is wrong, but not a social drink now and then. Charlie Dobbs sees this as a vital moral issue, and drinking is absolutely wrong. He has angrily challenged Bob, and the class has begun to take sides.[14]

9

Weapons, Strategies and How to Maintain Your Prayer Life

Heavenly Father, I come to You in the Name of my Lord and Savior, Jesus Christ. I come to You with praise and with thanksgiving, in worship, in humbleness to my Lord and Savior, Jesus Christ. Holy Spirit I ask You to reveal to me any un-confessed sins that I may have in my heart at this time. Heavenly Father, I ask You to forgive me and show me mercy from all sins known or unknown. I ask You Lord, to forgive me of all transgressions, iniquities, trespasses, any grudges or unforgiveness that I have in my heart at this time. Lord wash me clean with the Precious Blood of Jesus Christ. Lord Jesus, I ask You to destroy any assignments, plans or works that satan has against me. I ask You to cause Your anointing to break and destroy the yoke of every bondage that is over me and to bring down anything that exalts itself against the knowledge of God, as I take every thought captive to the obedience of Christ according to 2nd Corinthians 10:3-6. Lord Jesus I ask You to give me; freedom, and liberty from all sickness, and diseases and I ask You this according to Your complete and total Will, precious Jesus. Heavenly Father, I plead the Blood of Jesus Christ over me today. Lord, please help me to keep my eyes fixed on You, my Lord and Savior and to know that through You I am victorious. Lord, I ask You to release Your healing virtue into my body and to give me divine health. Lord Jesus I ask that You touch me and loose and encamp Your warring angels and ministering angels into my presence and keep me safe least I stumble they will catch me. Heavenly Father, I ask You to bless and prosper me according to Your divine Will. IN Jesus Name I pray. Amen! Website at www.christianword.org. (Christian Word Ministries)

Weapons, strategies and how to maintain your prayer life

Too much tongue wagging causes problems and devastation. It is vital that the tongue is tamed. Talking, too, hinders your and others' prayers and growth. James uses the tongue metaphors to illustrate how the tongue can cause major issues in life. James teaches that the tongue is a small member, but when out of control, it creates explosive disasters. He continues to metaphorically allege that the tongue is harder to tame than wild beasts and that it is filled with poison more venomous than vipers. He continues by explaining that the untamed tongue is restless, filled with poison and spews out blessings and curses because it will engage us to indulge in sin. However, the tongue can be tamed through prayer! Instead of falling prey to midnight issues, get a grip and use prayer as a weapon to maintain your life.

Prayer is a weapon that will kill the enemy. But your prayer must not be recited from a carnal mind and heart. Prayer must not be said to vengeance or as revenge because prayer itself, is a weapon when it is used correctly. We are to pray for ours and others deliverance. We are to pray that God keep our minds free from bondage and cleanse our hearts from unforgiveness, hatred and bitterness. Pray armed with the knowledge that the weapons of our warfare are not carnal, but mighty to the pulling down of strongholds (strongholds are things that are holding you back or hindering you, addictions, childhood issues, pornography, etc.) Additionally, strongholds are:

"Indulged known sin (Psa. 66:18; Isa. 59:1, 2). Willful disobe-dience to known commandments (Prov. 28:9). Selfishness (James 4:3). Unforgiving spirit (Matt. 5:22, 23; 6:12). Lack of faith (Heb. 11:6; James 1:6). Idols in the heart (Ezek. 8:5–18; 14:1–3)".[1]

Prayer and Praise

Prayer and praise are like making biscuits with plain flour and no baking powder. Without baking powder, the biscuits will not rise and become fluffy, but remain flat, heavy and stuck to the bottom of the pan. The same with prayer and praise. Without both, a Christian will remain flat with no expression of joy, heavy with the cares of the world and personal concerns, and remain stuck to the bottom by Satan's strategies and pitfalls. But when baking powder is added like prayer and praise, it complement the other. A praying Christian can soar to praise and praise takes you to worship, worship places you in the realm of the Spirit or in the presence of God. While in His presence, He will provide you with clear directions on how to proceed to tear down Satan's kingdom and build up His (God's) kingdom. Praise is a link to the heavenly throne of God.

Praise is linked to prayer...." The connection of thought is that we ask our heavenly Father for provision, pardon, and protection with great confidence, since we know that for him to give this to his children on the one hand is within his capacity, and on the other is in line with the character he shows when he deals with men—that is, his glory. This, therefore, is an actual instance of praise for God's power and glory coming in to undergird prayer for the fruits of both.[2]

Community Outreach

A community is a social group of any size whose members reside in a specific locality, share government, and have common cultural and historical heritage. Reach out and touch somebody's life. Touch is powerful: When parents lovingly and thoughtfully touch their children (hugs), they grow up feeling loved and will freely touch others; when premature babies are touched and cuddled while maturing in an incubator, they thrive and grow; when married couples touch each other, it implies, "I care about your emotional wellbeing."; but when we touch and agree in prayer, it sets God into motion on our behalf. The church lives to touch people, places, situations and communities. For example, the Englewood Community in Chicago, Illinois is continuing to struggle in many areas, but prayer and hope are impacting situations, people and things. A survey of the community revealed the following:

Community Type: Chicago Official Community Area
Longitude: -87.64
Latitude: 41.78
Land Area: 3.09 Square Miles
Per Capita Income (1999): $9,523
Typical Home Value: $60,114
Median Household Income: $19,513
Typical Rent (Monthly): $483.00
Median Year Homes Built: 1944 Total Population: 40,222

Crime is falling in Chicago, but one neighborhood hasn't felt that dip. According to the police department, in 2011, Englewood had more murders than any other police district in the city.

The Englewood police district clocked in more murders in 2011 than any other district. The area's crime problem is amplified because of other urban ills afflicting the neighborhood. Unemployment in and around Englewood is a whopping 35 percent. It's also one of the poorest enclaves in Chicago.

Relationship Status

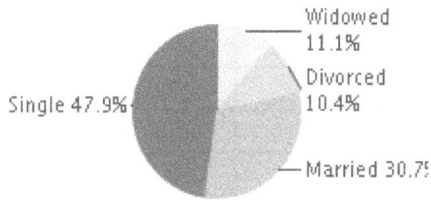

Widowed 11.1%
Divorced 10.4%
Single 47.9%
Married 30.7%

Homes with Kids

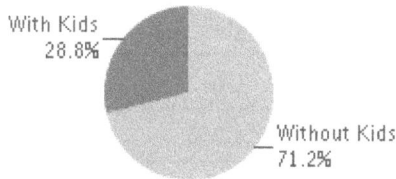

With Kids 28.8%
Without Kids 71.2%

Age Distribution

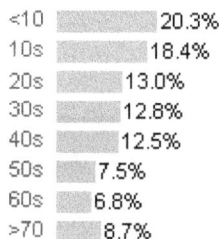

<10   20.3%
10s   18.4%
20s   13.0%
30s   12.8%
40s   12.5%
50s   7.5%
60s   6.8%
>70   8.7%

Commute Time

10 min or less	3.9%
10-20 min.	11.6%
20-30 min.	12.8%
30-45 min.	24.6%
45-60 min.	19.7%
60 min or more	27.3%

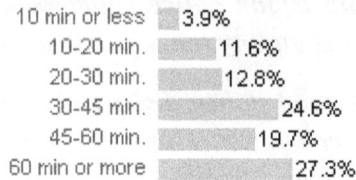

Englewood People Data

	Englewood	Chicago	National
Median Household Income:	$20,691	$38,625	$44,512
Single Males:	21.8%	21.0%	14.6%
Single Females:	26.0%	19.9%	12.5%
Median Age:	32	33	36
Homes With Kids:	28.8%	28.5%	31.4%
Average Household Size:	3.2	2.7	2.6
Average Commute Time (Minutes):	42	35	26

Race	Englewood
Caucasian	0.70%
African American	97.82%
Asian	0.35%
American Indian	0.12%
Native Hawaiian	0.01%
Mixed race	0.69%
Other race	0.31%

Education in this neighborhood (subdivision or community):
Percentage of people 3 years and older in K-12 schools:

Englewood:	29.4%
Chicago:	20.1%

Percentage of people 3 years and older in under-graduate colleges:

Englewood:	4.3%
Chicago:	5.6%

Percentage of people 3 years and older in grad. Or professional schools:

Englewood:	0.3%
Chicago:	2.0%

Percentage of students K-12 enrolled in private schools:

Englewood:	4.7%
Chicago:	16.7%

There are 31 schools in the Englewood community

Police officers/1000 residents	5.1
Total hospitals	1
Total churches	20^3

Prayer Walks in the Community

Do a community prayer walk in the Englewood Community? Of course we do. Many things have been discovered about the people in the community during evangelism and prayer walks. It was discovered that there are many things to pray about. Some things will move you to tears, others will cause rejoicing because of the love from the people in the community:

- Innocent children being killed on sidewalks

- A stray bullet through a closed window

- Mothers spending all their income and Link card allowance on things other than food and their children

- Abortions, same sex marriages, and lives destroyed by addictions

- False prophets, the spirit of pride and un-forgiveness

- A grieving mother, a broken marriage, a lost child

- Abandoned buildings

- Crack houses and un-kept apartment buildings

Cover the Community With Prayer

The on-going solution is to continue to cover the community with prayer and resources. It is a need to cover each community in and out of the Englewood community. The summer months present a good opportunity for the Women and Men groups to join in prayer walks and evangelism efforts. Whether inside or outside, the intercessory prayer ministry continues to bind the spirit of murder over the Chicago vicinity. Prayer is needed for the City and State level officials related to employment and housing issues for various communities. Men are eager to work. Let us continue to pray about it.

Assignment

Take a prayer walk through an urban (City) community of your choice

As you walk: Document the condition of the streets, apartment buildings, vacant lots, the street signs, what is going on in front of and inside the corner stores

- How many service stations and liquor store do you see?

- How are the community members interacting?

- Are there schools in the area?

- How many churches do you see that are open?

- Is there a laundromat in the community?

Ask the residents to tell you what the church is doing in the community?

www.trulia.com/englewood/community/chicago

www.wildonion.org/chicagoresource/englewood/information.htm.

www.theroot.com/chicago-murderrate

www.city.data.com/englewood/chicago/illinois.html

www.wbez.org/story/chicago-highest-murder-rate-englewood-95301

10

Prayer, A Strange Way to Fight

Prayer, a Strange Way to Fight

Don't wait until the battle is won to praise Him. Praise Him in the midst of the battle; Praise is what you do because of what God has done. Because we are in Christ and Christ is in us, we can do an "advance praise" dance before the Lord. An advance praise is uttering a thank you because we are winners through Jesus Christ. In His Army, there are no losers, only winners. Whether it's today or tomorrow, we are winners. Whether you were wounded, knocked down, pushed back, kicked or in a coma, you cannot and have not lost. Why? Because you are on the Lord's side and He is holding you during the battle. Think; prayer is a strange way to fight.

II Chronicles 20:1-26

It came to pass after this also, that the children of Moab, and the children of Ammon, and with them other beside the Ammonites, came against Jehoshaphat to battle. ² Then there came some that told Jehoshaphat, saying, There cometh a great multitude against thee from beyond the sea on this side Syria; and, behold, they be in Hazazon-tamar, which is En-gedi. ³ And Jehoshaphat feared, and set himself to seek the LORD, and proclaimed a fast throughout all Judah. ⁴ And Judah gathered themselves together, to ask help of the LORD: even out of all the cities of Judah they came to seek the LORD. ⁵ And Jehoshaphat stood in the congregation of Judah and Jerusalem, in the house of the LORD, before the new court, ⁶ And said, O LORD God of our fathers, art not thou God in heaven? and rulest not thou over all the kingdoms of the heathen? and in thine hand is there not power and might, so that none is able to withstand thee? ⁷ Art not thou our God, who didst drive out the inhabitants of this land before thy people Israel, and gavest it to the seed of Abraham thy friend forever?[1] *KJV*

The Problem

Jehoshaphat was faced with three armies that wanted to fight him. (Reference text above) Although, Jehoshaphat was fearful, he turned to the Lord in prayer. Not only did he pray, he invited other cities to join him. It is important to pattern situations after the acts of Jehoshaphat. He did not throw up his hands or give up, but he sought God through prayer. He called the congregation together and prayed. He talked out loud to the Lord and made his problem and desires known. When the devil is exposed in the presence of prayer, his power is removed from him so that no one hears the "personal business", instead, they hear the need to dismantle the enemies' power.

The Prayer

He called his people together and called for them to fast and pray. They needed to seek the Lord for help.

> *18 And Jehoshaphat bowed his head with his face to the ground: and all Judah and the inhabitants of Jerusalem fell before the LORD, worshipping the LORD. 19 And the Levites, of the children of the Kohathites, and of the children of the Korhites, stood up to praise the LORD God of Israel with a loud voice on high. KJV*

Jehoshaphat selected a prayer place, stood and bowed his face to the ground and humbly spoke openly to the Lord. The people mirrored their leader's behavior because their leader had a proven relationship with the Lord. Ask yourself, who will follow me when I am facing a battle, struggle, or the powers of darkness?

Sincere and heartfelt prayer leads praise into worship. The congregation stood and praised and worshipped the Lord with a loud voice. Read what happened next.

The Plan

> *20:22 - When they began to sing and to praise, the Lord set ambushments against the children of Ammon, Moab, and Mount Seir—KJV*

Jehoshaphat did not stay in bed, depressed, but he got up early in the morning to address the people, again. He was not overcome by his midnight, but forged ahead to day light. He reminded the waiting congregation to believe in the Lord, believe in his prophets, and believe that he has his instructions from the Lord. Imagine, he shared what the Lord had shared with him to the congregations. He had a praise team of singers to sing praises and worship the Lord in the "beauty of holiness" as they marched off to war. What did they sing? They sang, "No weapon formed against me will prosper", they chanted, "You are Lord, and we worship you", or maybe they simply sang, "Praise the Lord everybody". Are you able to sing a song in the midst of your adversity? The Lord heard their singing and set up the fight. Reminder: the fight was already fixed.

²² And when they began to sing and to praise, the LORD set ambushments against the children of Ammon, Moab, and mount Seir, which were come against Judah; and they were smitten. KJV

Look at the power of God and what happens when God sets and ambush for those who meant it for bad... He is in control of your midnight's outcome:

²⁴ And when Judah came toward the watch tower in the wilderness, they looked unto the multitude, and, behold, they were dead bodies fallen to the earth, and none escaped. KJV

²⁵ And when Jehoshaphat and his people came to take away the spoil of them, they found among them in abundance both riches with the dead bodies, and precious jewels, which they stripped off for themselves, more than they could carry away: and they were three days in gathering of the spoil, it was so much. ²⁶ And on the fourth day they assembled themselves in the valley of Berachah; for there they blessed the LORD: *therefore the name of the same place was called, The valley of Berachah, unto this day.* ²⁷ Then they returned, every man of Judah and Jerusalem, and Jehoshaphat in the forefront of them, to go again to Jerusalem with joy; for the LORD *had made them to rejoice over their enemies.* ²⁸ And they came to Jerusalem with psalteries and harps and trumpets unto the house of the LORD. ²⁹ And the fear of God was on all the kingdoms of those countries, when they had heard that the LORD *fought against the enemies of Israel.* ³⁰ So the realm of Jehoshaphat

was quiet: for his God gave him rest round about. *KJV*

The Power

20:24- when Judah came toward the watchtower in the wilderness there were dead bodies strewed all over the place. They never lifted a sword, a shield, a knife, or a stone to fight. The fight was fixed from the beginning. Why? Because Jehoshaphat and his people prayed for God to get the glory and the singers sang songs of victory before the battle was fought. That is what God is telling you (the reader). KJV

There is power in prayer and praise.

The Results: Victory in Battle

"*Ex 14:13* | *And Moses said unto the people, Fear ye not, stand still, and see the salvation of the LORD, which he will shew to you today: for the Egyptians whom ye have seen to day, ye shall see them again no more for ever.*

Ex 14:14 | *The LORD shall fight for you, and ye shall hold your peace.*

Jdg 7:22 | *And the three hundred blew the trumpets, and the LORD set every man's sword against his fellow, even throughout all the host: and the host fled to Beth-shittah in Zererath, and to the border of Abel-meholah, unto Tabbath.*

1 Sa 14:20 | *And Saul and all the people that were with him assembled themselves, and they came to the battle: and, behold, every man's sword was against his fellow, and there was a very great discomfiture.*

Ge 14:7 | *And they returned, and came to En-mishpat, which is Kadesh, and smote all the country of the Amalekites, and also the Amorites, that dwelt in Hazezon-tamar". (KJV)*

Obedience

The trumpets were blown and walls were broken down through

obedience. Obedience involves praying and paying attention to Jesus' call. Stop blaming others for your deficits and devote yourself to faithful prayer. We are to boldly proclaim His Holy Word. Devote yourself to faithful prayer. Follow the leaders Christ has placed in charge of your spiritual guidance. Live holy because you have become a new creature in Christ, practicing righteousness out of a pure heart. Obedience begins with sincere humbleness from an upright, watchful, truthful and zealous spirit for good works.

Order

Breakthrough by setting your spiritual house in order. In the book of Joshua, as soon as the people heard the sound of the trumpet, the people shouted a great shout, and the walls fell down flat. Then, the people went up into the city and captured it. In the book of Joshua, the people followed instructions and marched in order. In 2 Chronicles 20th chapter, the people prayed, sang, praised and worshipped before battle, in order. In both cases, God received glory and the people won the battle without one strike because they followed God's order through His leader.

Obtain

Take the city by devoting yourself to prayer and fasting during Midnight experiences. Remember, the adversary will make it seem like the nights are long and too difficult to endure, but the "battle is won because the fight is fixed". The first step is to get up and get started. Accept that Jesus has given you a plan and a way out. He will show you how to overcome obstacles to prayer.

Do you find prayer intimidating? Have you ever said, "I don't know how to pray"? If so, you may be surprised to learn that there is no "right" or "wrong" method of prayer and prayer is not reserved for a handful of religious professionals. If the wicked king Manasseh could cry out to God and be heard (2 Chr. 33:12–13), surely there is hope for the rest of us.

Problems that Jesus is Waiting to Work Out in Your Life

What's your woe? Sin and habits, grief, painful relationships, childhood hurt, disappointments, depression/sadness, unfaithfulness, marriage woes: woes of disrespect, cheating woe; lies woe; the dating game, lack of trust, children, domestic violence, substance abuse, disobedience, homosexuality, living a lie, caught in the act, starving for attention, fornication, adultery, unemployment, financial woes and chance takers: gambling, lottery, cards and other unhealthy habits. This is an ideal time to submit your ways, habits and unresolved issues to Jesus through prayer.

Assignment
(Self-Discovery Exercise)

11

Surveys, Interviews and Other Prayer Verifications

of Changes from Midnight to Daylight

He Whispered My Name

Jesus whispered my name. Ever since then, I haven't been the same.
His Name is Holy and it I proclaim. You see, Jesus whispered my
name. He didn't call loudly or in an outburst. It was not but like a soft
gentle voice. He whispered my name. "Feed my flock," He said. I'm
honored because He choose me. He didn't have to, He could have left
me blind, unable to see, but because of who He is, now I know because
when Jesus whispers your name forsake all and GO.
(By R. Messenger, 12/96)

Surveys, Interviews and Other Prayer Verifications of

Changes From Midnight to Daylight

The Wichita Eagle reports that the Kansas House OK's **prayer** room at state Capitol on:

*"Mar 28, 2012 called the Capitol **Prayer** and Meditation Room...*
*www.pewforum.org/.../Kansas-House-OKs-**prayer**-room-at-state-*
Capitol.

Wash. Post: Pope Francis slips into basilica for private prayer on first...

In his first morning as supreme pontiff and leader of the
world's 1.2 billion Catholics, www.pewforum.org/Pope-Francis-
*slips-into-basilica-for-private-**prayer**-on-first-full-day-as-pontiff.*
aspx -

Pew Forum: A prayer for the jobless

Jan 7, 2009 ... For people in Britain who have lost their
jobs - and for those who have seen colleagues laid off and are trou-
bled by feelings of guilt about still ...
*www.pewforum.org/Religion-News/A-**prayer**-for-the-jobless.aspx*

Tallahassee Democrat: Fla. House debates prayer - Pew Forum on...

Mar 2, 2012 ... By the time Florida House members ap-
proved a bill that will allow students to give inspirational messages
to their peers in school, supporters ...
*www.pewforum.org/Religion-News/Fla--House-debates-**prayer**.*

National Post: Church holds prayer day for Polish drivers - Pew...

Mar 31, 2011 ... The Roman Catholic Church in Poland
*will hold a day of **prayer** for the country's drivers, hoping to use*
the Christian spirit to quell road rage. www.pewforum.org/.../Na-
*tional-Post-Church-holds-**prayer**-day-for-Polish-drivers.aspx -*

Miami Herald: Senate approves school prayer bill - Pew Forum on...

> *Feb 1, 2012 ... Sen. Gary Siplin believes this is the year for school **prayer**.*
> *www.pewforum.org/.../Senate-approves-school-**prayer**-bill.aspx*

AP: Group sues to stop Texas governor's prayer day - Pew Forum...

> *Jul 13, 2011 ... A group of atheists and agnostics filed a federal lawsuit on Wednesday seeking to stop an evangelical Christian **prayer** event next month[1].*
> *www.pewforum.org/.../Group-sues-to-stop-Texas-governor-s-**prayer**-day.asp*

Toronto Star: Opinion: Siddiqui: A prayer for tolerance

> *Aug 20, 2011 ... The weekly Muslim **prayer** at a Toronto public school that's said to constitute an imminent threat to Canadian secularism has been going on for ...*
> *www.pewforum.org/Religion.../Siddiqui--A-**prayer**-for-tolerance.aspx -*

Pew Forum: UCLA Study: Students Become More Spiritual in College

> *Feb 14, 2008... Been examined here at the Pew Forum and elsewhere by measuring such things as attendance at religious services or frequency of **prayer**.*
> *www.pewforum.org/ucla-study-students-become-more-spiritual-in-college.aspx -*

CNN: Obama hosts Holy Week prayer breakfast - Pew Forum on...

> *Apr 19, 2011 ... President Obama held a **prayer** breakfast this morning at the White House, where he spoke about faith this Easter week.www.pewforum.org/.../Obama-hosts-Holy-Week-**prayer**-breakfast.aspx" -[23]*

Survey Form

What is your age range?

(13-19) (20-35) (36-49) (50-65) (66-80) (81-100) (Other)

1. How often do you pray? (3X's or more a day) (Daily) (Weekly) (Other)

2. Are you involved in a prayer ministry? (Yes) (No)

3. How do you minister to someone who declares privately to you that they are experiencing a bad situation? I.e. grief, financial troubles, joblessness, no income, no food, family problems, etc.)

4. How do you handle yours and others personal or private struggles? Possible strategies are as follows: Pray with them, give them money, encourage them to hold, provide transportation, connect with resources, make phone calls, refer them to someone else, or other.

5. Do your problems keep you awake at night?

6. Does your church have a formal prayer ministry? If so, are you actively engaged in the prayer ministry at your church?

7. What is your occupation?

8. Are you: employed, unemployed, a business owner operator, student, housewife, engaged in job search, or other?

9. Are you: married, single, divorced, widowed, separated, dating or other?

10. Please provide other information that you would like to share

Note: the information you have shared is personal and confidential. Your name will not appear in the published work. Thank you for sharing your information and thoughts with me.

Survey Form findings

1. A total of 43 individuals completed survey forms

2. 1 of the 43 was a 12-year old

3. 3 were ages 13-19; 2, 20-35; 9, 36-49; 20,50-65; and, 7,66-80

4. 10 prayed 3 or more times a day; 27 prayed daily; 1 prayed weekly and 2 prayed 2 times per day

5. 4 were involved in a prayer ministry; 6 had no involvement

6. How personal and private struggles were handled: 31 would pray with others; 7 would give money; 29 would encourage them to hold on; 9 would provide transportation; 18 would connect to resources; 11 would make phone calls; 6 would refer to someone else; and 1 would counsel or talk

7. Problems keep you awake: 14 said no; 3 says yes; 11 says sometimes; and 4 had no answer.

8. Does your church have a formal prayer ministry? 20 say yes; 15 say no; 1 says sometimes

9. Actively engaged in prayer ministry at church: 22 say yes; 15 say no and 5 had no answer

10. Occupations:

Home Care Provider, Maintenance, Retired (2), Medical Financial Counselor, Baby sitter at home, Construction, Caseworker, Laborer for Construction, Housekeeping, Accountant, RN-Administrator, Teacher, Investigator, and Pastor.

11. 19 Employed, 9 unemployed, 1 business owner, 9 students, 3 housewives, and 1 engaged in job search.

12. 16 married, 15 singles, 3 divorced, 3 widowed, and 2 separated

13. Other information you would like to share:

The general consensus is that the majority of the survey individuals (40 of 43) prayed one or more times per day, but few were involved in a formal prayer ministry.

12

Conclusion and Final Thoughts

Today, I Rise

Today, I rise;
no longer will I be bound to earthly sadness and sorrows.
Today I rise.
The negative, the unseen and the unredeemed will not have an adverse
effect on me, because Today, I rise.

Today I rise above my circumstances.
I rise above needless criticism.
I rise above and out of bondage.
I rise and I hoover above the things of the world;
my flesh and my fleshly desires.
I RISE.
I rise and give thanks, praise and worship to my Lord and Savior.
Today, I rise.
(By R. Messenger, 1996)

Conclusion and Final Thoughts

The darkness is not always good. Use your Midnight time to talk and listen to what the Lord is saying and how you are learning from your unwise choices. Begin on this wise:

- Re-focus your mind on things that are pleasing to God

- Review times that brought joy to your heart and insert a prayer of thanksgiving for the times

- Revise and develop plans of improvement that include purpose, goals and measures to accomplish them

- Repent of your sins and become godly sorrowful for not believing and trusting in Jesus

- Praise God for where you are. Thank Him that you are learning the lesson during your valley experience

- Worship in the spirit realm; while you are in that place with God, listen to Him and commit to view your ways that you will line up with His will for your life

- Learn the contents of the tool box, the Bible

- Recall His Word and stories of how God's people endured suffering and other issues

- Replay sermons and teachings literally and mentally for inspiration, guidance and affirmation that God is…

- Reclaim and/or establish a regular prayer life

- Re-align yourself with daylight, not darkness

- Reclaim your joy

- Rejoice in victory

- Restore or initiate your directions

- Release yourself from old habits

Again, exercise faith (faith is trusting God: Eph 2:8; Gal. 2:20; Col. 3:15; Rom. 1:17; Ps. 56:3), receive and repent

Prayer Changes Things

God can change anything through prayer according to His will.

Be anxious for nothing, but in everything by prayer and supplication, with thanksgiving, let your requests be made known to God; and the peace of God, which surpasses all understanding, will guard your hearts and minds through Christ Jesus." (Phil.. 4:6-7) KJV

Prayer changes things only for God's people because "all things work together for good to those who love God, to those who are called according to His purpose." (Rom. 8:26-28). "Everything by prayer" does not mean everything in the universe, but rather "all things that pertain to life and godliness" (2 Pet. 1:3-4, 11). The "life" refers to eternal life. We pray only for the change that has connection to God's plan of salvation.

However, this does not mean that we pray only for spiritual things. Prayer will certainly change material things, when that change has a spiritual value and benefit.

Prayer is not for satisfying physical and material lusts (Jas. 4:3). It does not mean that we cannot pray for material needs. Jesus taught us to pray, "Give us each day our daily bread and forgive us our trespasses." (Luke 11:3-4) The main purpose of prayer, however, is to help make things "turn out for salvation" (Phil. 1:19).

> *"The effective, fervent prayer of a righteous man avails much." (Jas 5:16) When a righteous man prays there are more changes than he could ever imagine or comprehend. "And the prayer of faith will save the sick, and the Lord will raise him up. And if he has committed sins, he will be forgiven." (Jas. 5:15) The sick person is not only healed but also saved.*[1]

Midnight praying is praying for release, relief and refocusing. It is praying while using your weapons of warfare. It is praying for total deliverance while pressing through your Midnight in prayer. It is praying for resolution of Midnight turmoil. Midnight is a time between night and day that may include loneliness, yet you are not alone at midnight. Midnight challenges are just that, "challenges"; name your midnight deliverance

"Can prayer change things? Does talking to God have any effect whatsoever on what happens? If we are sick, does asking God to heal us make a difference in whether we get better? If a friend has rejected the Lord, is there any point in pleading for his salvation? These are not just theological questions. Our trust in God is at stake. On one hand, the Bible assures us that the Lord answers prayer. On the other, it teaches that God is the sovereign Lord who knows and rules all things according to his perfect will.

So we ask again: Can prayer really change God's will? Does it really affect what happens in our lives and in the world? Or does it only affect us spiritually as we express our gratitude and dependence on God? Thoughtful Christians wrestle with this issue. Sometimes we conclude that prayer strengthens our souls but doesn't change the world. What's going to happen will happen whether we pray or not.

...the Bible does say prayer changes things. James 5:16 says, "The effectual, fervent prayer of a righteous man availeth much." The Bible provides scores of powerful examples of prayers being answered. People like Hezekiah, Moses, Joshua, David, Hannah, and Paul received specific answers to their prayers. Even the great leaders in the Bible believed God answers prayers. There are hundreds of verses showing them asking God to change things"[2].

In conclusion, trust God...His loves surrounds us. God's trust goes in before His name goes on. Trust or confidence should be installed on the inside of us before God's Name goes into (inside) of us. Trust placed in the wrong places and things lead to wrong directions. Trust and commitment in the work place yields a salary to pay debts... that is outside trust. Not trusting 10% of our earnings is not trusting God's Word that deals with the obligation to support the Ministry head and support earthly kingdom building. Trust is often entrusted to people to respond to daily needs, that's outside trust. Yet, there is no trust for God to select what is needed for our basic daily needs. Trust in

Law enforcement and the government to write fair and just laws is a way of life, but is the same trust in God to plead cases and supply legal representation during encounters of trouble.

Failure or lack of trust in God leads to an anorexic condition. We are His sheep, but when the sheep will not eat, it develops weight loss and eventually death resulting from starvation. Does God have anorexic sheep? There is a nutritional saying, "garbage in, garbage out". It rings true; no food, no nourishments. Insufficient nourishment leads to lack of energy, poor thinking, no desire to press forward, no interest in moving forward, no drive, no conversation and the person is ultimately dying while living. So it is when there is a failure to ingest the daily Word on a regular and consistent basis that we become spiritually unhealthy. Daily, we should include between meals healthy snacks of Bible Study, Intercessory Prayer, Sunday school, etc. Spiritually unhealthy saints' lives become filled with garbage. There is a breakdown of dietary needs (the gospel, praise, worship, etc.). Energy rapidly fails, praise diminishes, thinking is distorted, and cells are depleted of the required food and water—the food from the Word and the water of the Holy Spirit. Desires become fleshly, and positive thinking is replaced with negative and random thoughts. The forward drive is in reverse, faintness is felt and the vessel is dying spiritually while life goes on.

Finally, it occurs that man should always pray and not faint. Holy boldness is needed to lead as Moses, face giants like David, and support leaders like Deborah. Martin Luther King stood up and boldly spoke out, pastor's stand in boldness in spite of the odds, women are involved in ministry in spite of rejection and criticism and youth are boldly gathering to sing in groups, churches and community choirs. Pray for your boldness!

Assignment

Rom. 14–15 also lay down vital fellowship principles. Be sure to explore how we are to deal with differences in convictions. You can cover this material in a mini lecture, or use the case-history approach.

Apply

Ask each person to examine his or her own attitude, and prayerfully ask God to purge him or her of judgmentalism, making room only for love.[3]

Consider this:

- If you were to die at midnight tonight, where would your soul spend eternity?

- Name one thing that has moved you to tears within the past three days.

The Survey Form
Take the Challenge

Your age range:

	13-19
	20-35
	36-49
	50-65
	66-80
	81-100
	Other

How often do you pray?
[ ] 3X's or more a day; [ ] Daily; [ ] Weekly; [ ] other

Are you involved in a prayer ministry?
[ ] Yes   [ ] No [ ] Other

How do you minister to someone who declares privately to you that they are experiencing a bad situation? (I.e. grief, financial troubles, joblessness, no income, no food, family problems, etc.?)

How do you handle yours and/or others personal, or private struggles?

[ ]Pray about it or with them	[ ]Give money	[ ] Encourage them to hold on
[ ] Provide transportation	[ ] Make phone calls	[ ] Connect with resources
[ ] Ask them to talk with someone else (referral)	[ ] other	

Do you stay awake at night because of your problem(s)?
[ ] Yes   [ ] No [ ] Sometimes

Does your church have a formal prayer ministry?   [ ] Yes [ ] No

If so, are you actively engage.d in the prayer ministry at your church?
[ ] Yes [ ] No

What is your occupation?

Are you [ ] Employed, [ ] unemployed, [ ] a business owner/operator, [ ] a student, [ ] a housewife, [ ] engaged in job search, or [ ] other?

Are you - [ ] Married, [ ] Single, [ ] Divorced, [ ] Widowed, [ ] Separated, [ ] Dating or [ ] Other?

Other information that you would like to share:

Chart Exercise

What is your area of ministry?	What is it called in the Biblical text?	Are you functioning in your ministry area?
Facilitator (facilitation)	Worship Leader	
Saturator (saturation)	Praise/worship	
Maturation	Teaching	
Implementation	Disciple	
Emancipation	Freedom/Release/Deliverance	
Preparation	Devotional service	
Location	Where the Spirit leads	
Conversation	Counseling	
Stimulation	The Word expressed	
Participation	Helps	
Impartation	Prophetic	
Celebration	Worship	
Installation	Your connection	
Convocation	Where you are to assemble	

Overcoming Obstacles to Prayer

Do you find prayer intimidating? Have you ever said, "I don't know how to pray"? If so, you may be surprised to learn that there is no "right" or "wrong" method of prayer. Nor is prayer reserved for a handful of religious professionals. If the wicked king Manasseh could cry out to God and be heard (2 Chr. 33:12–13), surely there is hope for the rest of us.

Which of the following characterizes your situation?

• *You feel deep guilt for willful sin that perhaps has even ruined your own or someone else's life. See David's prayer after he committed the sins of adultery and murder (Ps. 51).*

• *You feel scared by responsibilities that seem totally beyond your skills and ability. Read Moses' "argument" with God (Ex. 3:1–4:17).*

• *You feel frustrated and angry as you read about local, national, and international conditions, wondering why God doesn't seem to be doing anything. Study the Book of Habakkuk.*

• *You are afraid of a family member's hostility over wrongs that you have committed. Hear Jacob calling out to God for safety from his brother Esau (Gen. 32:9–12; for the outcome, see Gen. 33).*

• *You have been threatened by a superior who thinks you are out to take over his power and position. Listen as David cries out to God while fleeing from Saul (Ps. 57, 142).*

• *You have experienced prejudice and even persecution for your religious convictions. Look at the prayer for boldness that the early church prayed after its leaders had been jailed and threatened (Acts 4:13–31).*

• *Your child is terribly afflicted and you feel powerless to help. Consider the Syro-Phoenician woman's appeal to Jesus for mercy (Matt. 15:21–28).*

• *You are troubled by a chronic physical malady and have not experienced healing. Read about Paul's three appeals to God to remove his ailment (2 Cor. 12:7–10).*

There is no single method for expressing oneself to God. The Lord is not only completely able to hear our arguments, pleas, and pain—He wants to! He also delights to hear our joys, praises, and ecstasies. So open your heart to God. Then give yourself to patient listening for His response.[1]

Footnotes

Internet - *Does Prayer Change Things?* by Steve on December 1, 2009 ·

Bounds, E. M .: E.M. Bounds On Prayer: Whitaker House, 1997

PEW Forum U.S. Religious Landscape Survey, 2008

MacArthur, John: *Alone With God*. Wheaton, Ill. : Victor Books, 1995

Wiersbe, Warren W.: *Prayer : Basic Training*. Wheaton, IL : Tyndale, 1988 [Luke 22:32]

The Holy Bible: English Standard Version. Wheaton : Standard Bible Society, 2001, S. Ps 51:1-19

The Holy Bible: English Standard Version. Wheaton : Standard Bible Society, 2001, S. 2 Co 12:1-10

Thomas Nelson Publishers: *What Does the Bible Say About--: The Ultimate A to Z Resource Fully Illustrated*. Nashville, Tenn. : Thomas Nelson, 2001 (Nelson's A to Z Series), S. 378

Kurian, George Thomas: *Nelson's New Christian Dictionary: The Authoritative Resource on the Christian World*. Nashville, Tenn. : Thomas Nelson Pubs., 2001

The Holy Bible: King James Version. 2009 (Electronic Edition of the 1900 Authorized Version.) (Mt 6:6–14). Bellingham, WA: Logos Research Systems, Inc.

Torrey, RA (1907). Studies in the life and teachings of our Lord (66). Los Angeles: Bible Institute of Los Angeles.

Boa, Kenneth: *Handbook to Prayer: Praying Scripture Back to God*. Atlanta : Trinity House, 1997, c1993

Webster Electronic Dictionary

Thomas Nelson Publishers: *What Does the Bible Say About--: The Ultimate A to Z Resource Fully Illustrated*. Nashville, Tenn. : Thomas Nelson, 2001 (Nelson's A to Z Series), S. 198

Thomas Nelson Publishers: *What Does the Bible Say About--: The Ultimate A to Z Resource Fully Illustrated*. Nashville, Tenn. : Thomas Nelson, 2001 (Nelson's A to Z Series), S. 199

Wiersbe, Warren W.: *Wiersbe's Expository Outlines on the New Testament*. Wheaton, Ill. : Victor Books, 1997, c1992, S. 742

(Why Marriage Matters, Third Edition Thirty Conclusions from the Social Sciences. Institute for American Values; New York, NY. 2011 (www.americanvalues.org)

Richards, Larry; Richards, Lawrence O.: *The Teacher's Commentary.* Wheaton, Ill. : Victor Books, 1987, S. 836

Fahlbusch, Erwin; Bromiley, Geoffrey William: *The Encyclopedia of Christianity.* Grand Rapids, Mich.; Leiden, Netherlands: Wm. B. Eerdmans; Brill, 1999-<2003. - "The Encyclopedia of Christianity is the first of a five-volume English translation of the third revised edition of Evangelisches Kirchenlexikon. Its German articles have been tailored to suit an English readership, and articles of special interest to English readers have been added. The encyclopedia describes Christianity through its 2000-year history within a global context, taking into account other religions and philosophies. A special feature is the statistical information dispersed throughout the articles on the continents and over 170 countries. Social and cultural coverage is given to such issues as racism, genocide, and armaments, while historical content shows the development of biblical and apostolic traditions. This comprehensive work, while scholarly, is intended for a wide audience and will set the standard for reference works on Christianity."--"Outstanding reference sources 2000", American Libraries, May 2000. Comp. by the Reference Sources Committee, RUSA, ALA, S. 3:540

Wood, D. R. W.: *New Bible Dictionary.* InterVarsity Press, 1996, c1982, c1962, S. 769

Wood, D. R. W.: *New Bible Dictionary.* InterVarsity Press, 1996, c1982, c1962, S. 769

Thomas Nelson Publishers: *What Does the Bible Say About--: The Ultimate A to Z Resource Fully Illustrated.* Nashville, Tenn. : Thomas Nelson, 2001 (Nelson's A to Z Series), S. 200

Thomas Nelson Publishers: *What Does the Bible Say About--: The Ultimate A to Z Resource Fully Illustrated.* Nashville, Tenn. : Thomas Nelson, 2001 (Nelson's A to Z Series), S. 264

Thomas Nelson Publishers: *What Does the Bible Say About--: The Ultimate A to Z Resource Fully Illustrated.* Nashville, Tenn. : Thomas Nelson, 2001 (Nelson's A to Z Series), S. 201

Soanes, C., & Stevenson, A. (2004). *Concise Oxford English dictionary* (11th ed.). Oxford: Oxford University Press.

Fahlbusch, E., & Bromiley, G. W. (1999-2003). Vol. 3: The encyclopedia of Christianity (45-46). Grand Rapids, MI; Leiden, Netherlands:

Wm. B. Eerdmans; Brill.

Fahlbusch, E., & Bromiley, G. W. (1999-2003). Vol. 3: The encyclopedia of Christianity (45-46). Grand Rapids, MI; Leiden, Netherlands: Wm. B. Eerdmans; Brill.

Myers, A. C. (1987). The Eerdmans Bible dictionary (986). Grand Rapids, MI: Eerdmans.

du Rand, J. (1998). Groups in Jewish national life in the New Testament period. In A. du Toit (Ed.), .Vol. 2: The New Testament Milieu (A. du Toit, Ed.). Guide to the New Testament. Halfway House; Orion Publishers.

du Rand, J. (1998). Groups in Jewish national life in the New Testament period. In A. du Toit (Ed.), .Vol. 2: The New Testament Milieu (A. du Toit, Ed.). Guide to the New Testament. Halfway House; Orion Publishers.

du Rand, J. (1998). Groups in Jewish national life in the New Testament period. In A. du Toit (Ed.), .Vol. 2: The New Testament Milieu (A. du Toit, Ed.). Guide to the New Testament. Halfway House; Orion Publishers.

Richards, Larry; Richards, Lawrence O.: *The Teacher's Commentary*. Wheaton, Ill. : Victor Books, 1987, S. 834

Merriam-Webster's Collegiate Dictionary; Eleventh Edition on CD-ROM; V. 3.1 2004 *(Merriam-Webster Electronic Collegiate Dictionary)*

Richards, Larry; Richards, Lawrence O.: *The Teacher's Commentary*. Wheaton, Ill. : Victor Books, 1987, S. 835

Spence-Jones, H. D. M. (Hrsg.): *The Pulpit Commentary: 2 Samuel*. Bellingham, WA : Logos Research Systems, Inc., 2004, S. 592

Zuck, Roy B.: *A Biblical Theology of the New Testament*. electronic ed. Chicago : Moody Press, 1994; Published in electronic form by Logos Research Systems, 1996, S. 361

African American Handbook by Floyd Flake

Zuck, Roy B.: *A Biblical Theology of the New Testament*. electronic ed. Chicago : Moody Press, 1994; Published in electronic form by Logos Research Systems, 1996, S. 362

Zuck, Roy B.: *A Biblical Theology of the New Testament*. electronic ed. Chicago : Moody Press, 1994; Published in electronic form by Logos Research Systems, 1996, S. 362

Willmington, H. L.: *Willmington's Bible Handbook*. Wheaton, Ill. : Tyndale House Publishers, 1997, S. 668

[h] ver. 2

The Holy Bible: English Standard Version. Wheaton : Standard Bible Society, 2001, S. Eph 5:25

MacArthur, John Jr: *The MacArthur Study Bible*. electronic ed. Nashville : Word Pub., 1997, c1997, S. Eph 5:25

The Holy Bible: English Standard Version. Wheaton : Standard Bible Society, 2001, S. Ro 5:12

Zuck, Roy B.: *A Biblical Theology of the New Testament*. electronic ed. Chicago : Moody Press, 1994; Published in electronic form by Logos Research Systems, 1996, S. 358

Zuck, Roy B.: *A Biblical Theology of the New Testament*. electronic ed. Chicago : Moody Press, 1994; Published in electronic form by Logos Research Systems, 1996, S. 365

Bounds, Edward M.: *Power Through Prayer*. Oak Harbor, WA : Logos Research Systems, Inc., 1999

Richards, Larry; Richards, Lawrence O.: *The Teacher's Commentary*. Wheaton, Ill. : Victor Books, 1987, S. 837

Christian Word Ministries), 428 Southland Drive, Lexington, Kentucky 40503. Richard Broadbent, III, Christian Word Ministries Producer of "Prayers";_ *"The little Red Prayer Book: March 27, 1937; March 29, 2010*

Evans, William; Coder, S. Maxwell: *The Great Doctrines of the Bible*. Enl. ed. Chicago : Moody Press, 1998, c1974, S. 176

Packer, J. I.: *Growing in Christ*. Wheaton, Ill. : Crossway Books, 1996, c1994, S. 208

www.trulia.com/englewood/community/chicago

www.wildonion.org/chicagoresource/englewood/information.htm.

www.theroot.com/chicago-murderate

www.city.data.com/englewood/chicago/illinois.html

www.wbez.org/story/chicago-highest-murder-rate-englewood-95301

The *Holy Bible: King James Version*. 2009 (Electronic Edition of the 1900 Authorized Version.) (2 Ch 20). Bellingham, WA: Logos Research Systems, Inc.

www.pewforum.org/.../Group-sues-to-stop-Texas-governor-s-prayer-day.asp Toronto Star: Opinion: Siddiqui: Prayer for tolerance

http://www.pewforum.org/press-room/pew-forum-in-the-news

http://www.pewforum.org/press-room/pew-forum-in-the-news

(Arkwriter: http://arkwriter.hubpages.com)

(Michael Bronson, 1998, Biblehelp.org, Salvation – 2005)

Richards, Larry; Richards, Lawrence O.: *The Teacher's Commentary.* Wheaton, Ill. : Victor Books, 1987, S. 838

Thomas Nelson Publishers: *What Does the Bible Say About--: The Ultimate A to Z Resource Fully Illustrated.* Nashville, Tenn. : Thomas Nelson, 2001 (Nelson's A to Z Series), S. 314

Bibliography
Websites

"Welcome to Bullying Statistics." Bullying Statistics. N.p., n.d. Web. Feb.-Mar. 2012. <http://www.bullyingstatistics.org/>.

"Welcome." Mental Health America: N.p., n.d. Web. 15 Sept. 2012. <http://www.nmha.org/>.

"Terms and Conditions." Welcome to Facebook. Mark Zuckerberg, n.d. Web. 22 Sept. 2012. <http://www.facebook.com/>.

"Gay Bullying Statistics." - Bullying Statistics. N.p., n.d. Web. 9 Oct. 2012. <http://www.bullyingstatistics.org/content/gay-bullying-statistics.html>.

Articles

Friedman, Reva. "Blending Support and Social Action: The Power of a Gay-straight Alliance and Prideworks Conference." Secondary Gifted Education (2006) Print

Norton, Terry L., and Jonathan W. Vare. "Understanding Gay and Lesbian Youth: Sticks, Stones, and Silence." 17 July 1998: 3

Garofalo, R. Wolf, R.C., Kessel, S., Palfrey., J (1998) Pediatrics, 101 (5), 895-902

Chase, Anthony. "Violent Reaction; What do Teen Killers have in Common?" In These Times. 9 July 2001

Bart, M. Creating a safer school for gay students. Counseling Today, September 1998

Sessions Stepp, Laura. "A Lesson in Cruelty: Anti-Gay Slurs Common at School; Some Say Insults Increase as Gays' Visibility Rises." The Washington Post 19 June 2001

Waldo CR, Hesson McInnis MS, D'Augelli AR. Antecedents and consequences of victimization of lesbian, gay, and bisexual young people: a structural model comparing rural university and urban samples. Am J Community Psychol. 1998; 26:307–334.

Bontempo DE, D'Augelli AR. Effects of at-school victimization and sexual orientation on lesbian, gay, or bisexual youths' health risk behavior. J Adolesc Health. 2002; 30:364–374

Ruggiero KM, Taylor DM. Coping with discrimination: how disadvantaged group members perceive the discrimination that confronts them. J Pers Soc Psychol. 1995; 68:826–838.

PEW Forum U.S. Religious Landscape Survey, 2008
Website at www.christianword.org. Christian Word Ministries, 428 Southland Drive, Lexington, Kentucky 40503. Richard Broadbent, III, Christian Word Ministries Producer of "Prayers"; "The little Red Prayer Book: March 27, 1937; March 29, 2010

Appendices, Solutions & Strategies, Chapter Overview, Tables & Illustrations

Christian Growth

From the table below, find yourself. Select **"yes"** or **"no"** for the area(s) that is/are hindering your **Christian growth**. (The list is not comprehensive, but an example)

Y/N	What	Y/N	What	Y/N	What	Y/N	What	Y/N
	Laziness		Attitude		Unmotivated		Envy	
	Unfaithfulness		Pride		Guilt		Self-Absorption	
	Un-forgiveness		Unbelief		Bitterness		Jealously	
	Gossip		Love		Fear		Denial	
	People		Greed		Hatred		Low Self-Esteem	
	Hurt		No Prayer		Selfishness		Rebellion	
	Habits		Unhealthy Desires		Lying		Shame	
	Hostility		Judgment		Stubbornness		Weights	
	Grief		Excuses		Anxiety		Depression	
	Anger		Fault Finder		Procrastinator		Poor Study Habits	

The next step

1. Ask God to give you a hunger and thirst for His Word

2. Ask Jesus to make your decisions for you and begin the change needed to change your life

Solutions and Strategies for Praying through Your Midnight

Pray and ask God to:

1. "Fix me Jesus"

2. Change my mind

3. Instill steadfastness in me

4. Help me pray through

5. Teach me how to become spiritually healthy

6. Send mentoring help

7. Help me break the cycle

8. Positive self-talk

9. Use treatment from the Word

10. Change my friends and places

11. Ground me in the Word

12. Ask, "Is there anything too hard for God?"

13. Help me to become people friendly

14. Help me to become angry with the enemy and enraged by his tactics

15. Teach me how to pamper yourself

16. Dine on the Word, feast on prayer, press in praise, and win through worship

17. How to do it...

18. Help me remain consistent – stick to it

19. Help me to keep the faith – know that God is…

20. For help from prayer ministry (those who are committed and diligent in the ministry of intercession).

21. Teach me how to praise in spite of …

22. Help me to sing unto the Lord

23. Teach me how to surround yourself with saved people who believe in the ministry of prayer

24. Show me how to seek wise counsel from your spiritual leaders

25. Not to allow me to isolate myself from others

26. Adjust my attitude – put on a happy face

27. Teach me how to fast for power and strength

28. Teach me to journal your concerns, blessings, and desires

29. Teach me how not to doubt His ability and deliver you during your dark times in life

30. Teach me how to forgive, forget and forge ahead

31. Let go of bitterness, anger and resentment

32. How not to blame others

33. Pay my tithes and give an offering; support the ministries of your own church

34. Read the Bible within the context of the text

35. Attend teaching classes weekly

36. Put on the whole armor of God

37. Demonstrate the fruit of the Spirit

38. Become an active member of the prayer ministry

39. Evangelize with boldness

40. Saturate my home with praise music and spirit-filled teaching and preaching

41. Connect with friends

42. Implement a Christian book reading ministry

43. Attend group meetings (Christ – centered)

44. Read the 23rd Psalms until you believe it

Chapters Overview

Praying Through Your Midnight

Goal: "Praying Through Your Midnight" is written to help develop and provide a documented composite that describes how persistent prayer changes people, locations and situations

Purpose: To encourage the saints and inspire the general population to pray without ceasing through midnight experiences

Chapter One: Introduction: Praying While Others are Asleep? Who Needs Prayer?

Introduction that speaks to the ability to begin praying while others are asleep and asks the question, "Who needs prayer?" It concludes with comments on how prayer changes people and continues with how prayer changes locations and situations. The chapter ends with an assignment.

Chapter Two: Prayer, What Is It?

This chapter explores the meaning, purpose, and effect of prayer. It includes the need to change, and measures to enlighten and help build up the body of Christ. Examples of prayer from the Biblical text by David, Jesus and Paul. There is information on how one is changed through spiritual warfare by taking territories, removing generational curses and familiar spirits and binding the enemy and his works. The chapter concludes with "Lord teach me how to pray" by Dr. Bertha Shavers, Homewood, IL and an assignment.

Chapter Three: Midnight: A Time of Great Darkness

This chapter introduces real life midnight situations and the darkness and depression that follows. The midnight may be a time of loneliness and feeling of abandonment that requires pressing through the darkness until the midnight is over because it leads to poor and uninformed choices. The chapter ends with a riveting affirmation by Pastor Herbert Lee, Jr., Chicago, IL and an assignment.

Chapter Four: A Call to Holiness (I Peter 1:13-16)

In case there is an unawareness of how to prepare your mind for living Holy, step one is to ground your hope in holiness, conform to Christ-centered living, understand the call to live holy, conduct yourself as becoming holiness, and encouragement through prayerful diligence by a committed teenager, Amina Latrice James, Chicago, IL and an assignment.

Chapter Five: Prayer Stirs the Lives of People

This chapter teaches the importance of learning how to pray, how to become involved and convicted, and the need to practice ceaseless prayer. The chapter concludes with an engaging illustration of how prayer stirs people and sets change in motion by Pastor Author James Felton, Chicago, IL. An overview of prayer in government, in families and in churches and an assignment.

Chapter Six: Prayer Will Place One in Ministry

In this segment, there is encouragement to start where you are, challenge yourself to find your secret place and change your location. There is information on your selection of a place of ministry and ministering location that will facilitate change through prayer and an assignment.

Chapter Seven: Sincere Prayer Changes Midnight Situations

Learn about midnight situations, the Holy Spirit's inspiration and how the midnight situation is dissolved through prayer. Read about examples from real lives, examples from the Biblical text and situations changed through prayer by a proliferating Intercessor, Mildred J. Bonds, Chicago, IL and an assignment.

Chapter Eight: When Men Pray, a Change Will Come

The results of Pastor's empowering men to pray and man's responsibilities from the text in real life situations and how the church is holding men responsible for returning to church and ministry. The final phase of the chapter presents an illumination of Moving Men, Ministries and Mending Communities by an astute business man with powerful insight into the movement of people and ministries, Apostle H. L. Messenger and an assignment.

Chapter Nine: Weapons, Strategies and How to Maintain Your Prayer Life
Presents a simple portrayal of how community outreach and prayer walks in community are important ways to cover the community with prayer and an assignment.

Chapter Ten: Prayer, A Strange Way to Fight
A selected text from the Book of Chronicles is used to present the Problem, the Prayers, the Plan, the Power and the Results which is "Victory". It concludes with providing how to accept Jesus and His plan for the way out followed by an assignment.

Chapter Eleven: Surveys, Interviews and Other Prayer Verifications of Change From Midnight to Daylight

Chapter Twelve: Conclusion and Final Thoughts

Tables and Illustrations

Tables

1. Satan's Characteristics

2. A Survey of the Community

3. Survey Form

4. Chart Exercise

5. Christian Growth Exercise

Testimonials & Affirmations

"Lord Teach Me How To Pray: Effective and Prevailing Prayer" by Dr. Bertha Shavers, South Holland, IL

Walking Thru Midnight With A Prayerful Attitude

by Pastor Herbert Lee, Jr., Sr. Pastor of New Progressive Baptist Church; Chicago, IL (Married to Naomi Tobias-Lee)

Encouragement to Embrace Holiness from a Teenager's Perspective

The Question: To what extent can a gay teenager develop a plan for peace while using Facebook from 3:00pm until 11:00pm? by an eighteen (18) year old, Amina L. James, YAT (Youth and Teen) Ministry of Holy Rock Church & Outreach Ministries, Chicago, IL

Prayer Stirs People and Sets Change in Motion

by Pastor Author James Felton, Sr. Pastor of New Revelation of Holiness Baptist Church, Chicago, IL (Married to Drusilla Felton)

The Situation Changed Through Prayer – "My Midnight"

by Mildred J. Bonds, Intercessor, Holy Rock Church & Outreach Ministries, Chicago, IL 60621

Moving Men, Ministries and Mending Communities

by Apostle H. L. Messenger, Sr. Pastor Holy Rock Church & Outreach Ministries & CEO of Holy Rock Outreach Ministries, Inc.

Glossary

Block quotations. Quoted material set off typographically from the text by indention.

Boldface type. Type that has a darker and heavier appearance than regular type (like this)

Italic type. Slanted type suggestive of cursive writing (like this), as opposed to roman type.

Lowercase letters. An uncapitalized letter of a font (a, b, c, etc.)

Roman numeral. A numeral formed from a traditional combination of roman letters, either capitals (I, 11, 11, etc.) or lowercase (i, ii, iii, etc.)

Roman type. The primary type style (like this), as opposed to italic type

Run-in quotations. Quoted material set continuously with text, as opposed to a block quotation.

Special "Thank You"

A special "thank you" to the Professors of the satellite site "In His Image School of Ministry" for Martha's Vineyard Theological Seminary for doctoral studies instructions. Thank you to a phenomenal group of Instructors:

IN HIS IMAGE SCHOOL OF MINISTRY
Garfield Park Community Worship Center
4100 W. Jackson Blvd. ~ Chicago, IL 60624
www.inhisimageschool.org

Founder/Dean of Students:
Rev. Dr. E. Stephen Roberts

Professor Katheryn Roberts
Professor Richard Watson
And volunteers

Other
LIVING IMAGE PUBLISHING
Publications

Beyond the Flesh
Rev. Dr. E. Stephen Roberts

Heirs of Desiny: Being Black & God's Elect
Rev. Dr. E. Stephen Roberts
www.heirsofdestiny.com

www.livingimagepublishing.org
Chicago, Illinois

Holy Rock Church & Outreach Ministries

5854 S. Morgan Street
Chicago, IL 60621
Office: 773.471.0300
Email: holyrock936@gmail.com
Apostle H. L. Messenger, Sr. Pastor & Ministries Overseer

Classes/Ministries

Sunday
Morning Glory Hour - 8:00 a.m.
Sunday for all ages & Christian Foundation Class for New Members–
9:00 a.m.
Children's Church & Morning Worship – 10:45 a.m.

Saturday
The Women's Enrichment Ministry (The WEM) every 1st and 3rd
Saturdays at 9:00 a.m.
Minister's Meeting – 10:00 a.m.
Sunday School Teacher's Meeting last Saturday of each month at 9:00
a.m.
Intercessory Prayer Ministry Sunday – 10:30 a.m. and Saturday 9:00
a.m.

Wednesday
Pastor's Meeting 10:30 a.m.
Noon Day Bible Study (12:00 p.m.)
Leadership Class   6:00 p.m.
Monthly Deacon's Meeting 5:30 p.m.
Music Ministry Rehearsal 6:00 p.m.
Bible Study 7:00 p.m.

Every Third Wednesday
Iron Sharpens Iron Men Ministry
Family Ministry
Single's Ministry Meeting

www.ingramcontent.com/pod-product-compliance
Lightning Source LLC
LaVergne TN
LVHW091254080426
835510LV00007B/265